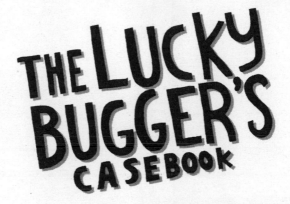

THE LUCKY BUGGER'S CASEBOOK

Tales of Serendipity and Outrageous Good Fortune

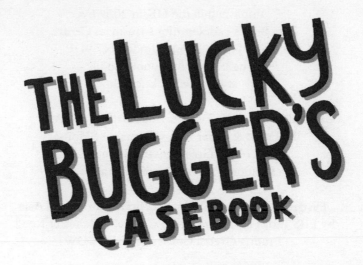

THE LUCKY BUGGER'S CASEBOOK

Tales of Serendipity and Outrageous Good Fortune

Daniel Smith

ICON BOOKS

Published in the UK in 2009 by
Icon Books Ltd, Omnibus Business Centre,
39–41 North Road, London N7 9DP
email: info@iconbooks.co.uk
www.iconbooks.co.uk

Sold in the UK, Europe, South Africa and Asia
by Faber & Faber Ltd, Bloomsbury House,
74–77 Great Russell Street,
London WC1B 3DA or their agents

Distributed in the UK, Europe, South Africa and Asia
by TBS Ltd, TBS Distribution Centre, Colchester Road,
Frating Green, Colchester CO7 7DW

Published in Australia in 2009
by Allen & Unwin Pty Ltd, PO Box 8500,
83 Alexander Street, Crows Nest, NSW 2065

Distributed in Canada by Penguin Books Canada,
90 Eglinton Avenue East, Suite 700,
Toronto, Ontario M4P 2YE
ISBN: 978-184831-080-3

Contents

About the author

Daniel Smith works in publishing as a researcher, writer and editor of non-fiction (including *The Statesman's Yearbook*, a geo-political guide to the world, *The Artist's Yearbook* and *The Screenwriter's Handbook*), and in 2003 lived and worked in Calcutta, India. He is the author of *World in Your Pocket*, a factbook about the countries and cultures of the world, and *The Sherlock Holmes Companion: An Elementary Guide*. He lives in east London with his partner, Rosie, and an assortment of fish.

For Rosie

Acknowledgements

This book was highly enjoyable to put together, and for that I owe a debt of gratitude to several people. Firstly to my editor, Duncan Heath, for all his suggestions and encouragement, and to the team at Icon. Also to all those friends and acquaintances who have offered up so many gems of serendipity for consideration. Particular thanks to my crack team of dedicated researchers (you know who you are!) and to Rosie, my own personal proof that good luck can happen to anyone.

Introduction

Serendipity *n.* the faculty of making happy and unexpected discoveries by accident

(The Concise Oxford Dictionary)

For most of us, serendipity seems to go out of its way to avoid our company. We aren't that person who finds a lottery ticket on the pavement and wins a million. We weren't singing to ourselves on the back of the bus when the record producer sat down on the seat in front. We didn't buy that rather twee landscape at the car boot sale only to find there was a Michelangelo sketch on the back.

It was Horace Walpole, that great 18th-century connoisseur of the English language and son of Prime Minister Robert Walpole, who coined the word 'serendipity'. Its origins lie in an ancient Persian fairytale, *The Three Princes of Serendip*, the story of three brothers sent by their father to Serendip (the Persian name for Sri Lanka) so that they might increase their knowledge of the world and their wisdom. Walpole defined his new word as the process by which people make 'discoveries, by accident and sagacity, of things which they were not in quest of', just as the princes did during their many adventures.

So it is that serendipity isn't *simply* a case of good luck, but rather the instance of an unsought-for opportunity of which one is able to take advantage. Take one of the most famous cases of serendipity in history: Newton seeing an apple fall from a tree – this was almost certainly what happened, rather than the oft quoted tale of an apple falling on his head – and developing his theory of gravity from the observation. Now, had Newton already had the germ of his theory and thought that he might be able to validate it by contemplating an apple tree, we might have considered it a big stroke of luck when the apple fell right there in front of him, providing him with the proof he needed. It's the fact that he just happened to see the apple fall, and that this unbidden occurrence prompted his theory, that makes the story a classic example of serendipity.

The other key component of Walpole's definition is 'sagacity'. To be 'sagacious', according to the *Oxford Concise Dictionary*, is to be 'mentally penetrating; gifted with discernment; having practical wisdom'. Let's look at Newton again. How many millions of people had seen apples falling from trees before Newton? Yet it was he who had the far-sighted wisdom to take advantage of the opportunity presented by the falling apple and turn it into something meaningful (his theory). Not everyone in this book can claim to have had the vision of Newton, but the very fact that their individual stories came to light shows that, even if the full significance of their chance discoveries eluded them, they at least had the sense that they were on to something.

Many of the anecdotes in this book are serendipitous in the purest sense. A lot tell of individuals who discovered something – an idea, a product, a thing that was long lost – when they hadn't been looking for it in the first place. As Walpole noted, 'many discoveries have been made by men who were à la chasse of something very different'. In other stories, I have treated the idea of 'discovery' in its widest sense, so that it might take the form of an opportunity for fame or fortune or, in the case of the 'Great Escapes' chapter, the opportunity of life itself. Another chapter, 'Criminal Negligence', describes notable instances where it was the forces of law and order that were the beneficiaries of serendipity, solving crimes with unexpected ease because of levels of stupidity or incompetence by criminals that could never have been predicted.

In gathering together this small collection of serendipity and chance, I have included some examples that made but a small impression on our world and others that have come to affect it fundamentally. It's possible that a few of the tales have been embellished through the mists of time, but each of them has a basis in fact. In all cases, the end result isn't the predictable outcome of a logical chain of events but is instead rooted in that rare and precious thing: a little bit of unsolicited good luck. As Ovid wrote: 'Luck affects everything; let your hook always be cast; in the stream where you least expect it, there will be a fish.'

Daniel Smith

CHAPTER 1

Inventions and Innovations (Part 1)

Some of the world's greatest inventions came about when inventors left the cul de sac of their original idea to stumble down a dark alleyway of innovation. The ability to recognise the appearance of unexpected opportunity is testament to the flexibility of the human mind and is something to be celebrated. The mystery writer Lawrence Block once noted: 'One aspect of serendipity to bear in mind is that you have to be looking for something in order to find something else.'

In the heat of the moment

Christopher Columbus introduced Europe to rubber after he witnessed it being used as a bouncy toy by the indigenous population of Haiti. It was only around 1770 that the substance became known as India rubber, when its effectiveness at removing pencil marks was discovered. Yet while the tough, flexible material had obvious potential, it was let down by a fundamental weakness: it didn't fare well in extreme weather conditions. On a hot, sunny day rubber would melt and decompose, and in the icy cold it froze rigid. The race was on to discover a way to make it more durable. Charles Goodyear would emerge triumphant following a small mishap in his kitchen.

Charles Goodyear was born in New Haven, Connecticut in 1800. The family had a background in the hardware business, but things had gone badly for them and Charles found himself burdened with debt while still a young man. He was even in a debtors' prison for a time. But by the early 1830s Goodyear had become convinced that there was a fortune to be made by improving rubber's resilience, and he set his mind to the task. However, his initial treatments using magnesia and then nitric acid proved to be false dawns and he soon ran out of business partners, who became weary of his trial-and-error approach.

Then came a breakthrough, though not of his own making. He learned (possibly by the use of threats) from another inventor, Nathaniel Hayward, that rubber seemed to benefit from the addition of sulphur. Goodyear now had a new direction down which to go. One day in 1839 he was boiling up a lump of rubber in a sulphur solution on a stove belonging to his wife, Clarissa, when the secret of vulcanisation revealed itself to him. He inadvertently dropped a blob of the gummy mixture directly onto the red-hot stove and saw at once that, at this extreme temperature, the rubber retained all of its flexibility and strength without melting or deteriorating. The vulcanisation process essentially took the loose molecules of the rubber, which naturally slid over each other, and locked them into place.

The process has barely changed to this day, and it ensured that rubber became a key component in countless industrial innovations. Yet Goodyear's discovery didn't provide him with the wealth and happiness that might have been expected. It took him until 1844 to be granted a patent, and those years spent perfecting the process were lived in near-poverty. The remainder of his life was dogged by legal challenges to his patent. The struggles took a toll on his health and for his last six years he could walk only with the aid of crutches. He died in 1860, over $200,000 in debt. His name, though, has gone on via the Goodyear Tire & Rubber Company, founded in 1898 by Frank Seiberling and named in honour of the great innovator.

Field of vision

Philo T. Farnsworth was pivotal to the development of television, inventing the first completely electronic television system. He demonstrated it in 1928 but the idea had first come to him eight years earlier, as a fourteen-year-old boy ploughing a potato field in Idaho.

Farnsworth was born into a Mormon family in Utah and showed an early interest in mathematics and technology. In 1912 the family set up home on a ranch in Rigby, Idaho. It was here that he was tilling a field when the idea of electronic television came to him. In a moment of unplanned inspiration, he surveyed the neat system of furrows produced by his horse-drawn plough and saw that, in the same way, an image might be scanned line-by-line and sent electronically through the airwaves before being reassembled line-by-line by a receiving device.

Farnsworth rushed into school to share his ideas with one of his teachers, filling a blackboard with detailed drawings and mathematical workings-out. It took several years for Farnsworth to develop a working system as he set about finding investors and establishing a research laboratory in San Francisco. In September 1927, still only 21 years old, he demonstrated his system to his backers, electronically transmitting the image of a straight line scratched into a black glass slide. A year later he showed the system to a select group of journalists. Up until then, television pioneers like John Logie Baird had relied on mechanical systems that would only ever be able to produce relatively low-resolution images.

For much of the early 1930s Farnsworth was occupied by a bitter patent dispute with the Radio Corporation of America and one of its developers, Vladimir Zworykin. Farnsworth's old science teacher, Justin Tolman, was called upon to produce the sketches Philo had done for him as a fourteen-year-old, which proved how the invention had been in his mind all those years. It was a clinching piece of evidence and Farnsworth won the case in 1935.

Alas, Philo didn't benefit as he should have, not least because the Second World War denied him vast sales and his patent ran out shortly afterwards. One of the great mathematical minds of his generation, he was responsible for many other inventions including radar equipment, an infrared telescope, and 'fusors' used in the study of fusion reactions. Television, though, was always something of a disappointment to him, his son revealing that he believed it never showed anything 'worthwhile'.

Photographic prints

As long ago as the 14th century, there was an understanding that no two fingerprints were the same. However, it wouldn't be until the later part of the 19th century that serious progress was made in using them for criminal identification. The science of fingerprinting developed rapidly over the next 100 years. In 1979 it fell to a police photographer in Northampton to make a chance discovery that would propel the technology forward again.

The British authorities in India had been using fingerprints for administrative purposes for several decades when, in 1886, one Dr Henry Faulds suggested to Scotland Yard in London that they might be used in criminal cases too. Calcutta opened the world's first criminal fingerprinting bureau in 1897 and Scotland Yard followed suit four years later. In 1902 Harry Jacks became the first man to be convicted in a British court on fingerprint evidence when he was found guilty of burglary. In 1905 two brothers, Alfred and Albert Stratton, were the first to be convicted of murder.

Fingerprints are categorised as being one of two types: patent or latent. A patent print is easy to spot because it appears on a surface in a third-party substance, such as blood or paint. Latent prints, however, aren't apparent to the naked eye and must be detected by adding some kind of reagent to highlight the ridge patterns left by the natural secretions of the skin.

There are hundreds of different methods available to the modern forensic scientist but one of the most effective came courtesy of Laurie Wood, a forensics man with the Northampton police. Despite a knowledge of fingerprinting, he was working on entirely unrelated business on our fateful day. He had been taking photographs for the police and was processing the images using a small black developing tank. Wood spotted a crack in one side of it and set about repairing the damage with some common-or-garden superglue. Having let it set for a while, he returned to the tank and noticed something rather strange. There was a series of chalky white marks around the crack, among which was a set of his crystal-clear fingerprints. He realised that the fumes from the glue must have combined with moisture from the tank to form polymers visible to the human eye.

His forensic background kicking in, Wood quickly grasped the implications of this unexpected reaction. He took his discovery to his seniors and the method was put through thorough scientific tests. It was found that at the right temperature and humidity, everyday superglue would produce a white polymer layer when it came into contact with the moisture inherent in a fingerprint. Previously, latent fingerprint detection had relied on the application of a variety of different powders. Quickly adopted by the Home Office

Police Scientific Development Branch, Wood's process established itself as one of the most reliable methods of print identification available, and is today used by forces throughout the world.

Keeping it together

Velcro is the trademarked name for 'hook-and-loop' fastenings that, like Sellotape or the Hoover, has assumed the status of a generic name. With the ability to cheaply and effectively bond a huge array of different materials together on a temporary basis, it has proved a boon in fields as far apart as fashion and space exploration. Its invention was the direct result of a Swiss man noticing that his trousers were covered in burrs (seed cases of the burdock plant) after a walk in the countryside.

In 1941 George de Mestral, an engineer from the town of Commugny, embarked on his fateful hunting trip in the Swiss Alps with his dog. When he returned home, de Mestral saw that not only his trousers but also the fur of his dog were, rather annoyingly, peppered with burdock burrs. The scientist in de Mestral took over and he placed the burrs under his microscope. He saw how they had tiny 'hooks' that attached themselves to any available 'loops', whether in the material fibres of his clothing or on his canine friend's coat. He realised that this system could have practical applications and turned his mind to developing a system of artificial hooks and loops that might, for instance, be able to do the job of a zip.

His early prototypes used cotton but proved not to be very durable. After a great deal of experimentation he decided to use Nylon, which produced perfect loops when woven and heat-treated. The question of the hooks was somewhat more difficult until de Mestral realised that he could form them simply by cutting the hoops in just the right place. He came up with the name Velcro for his creation by combining the French words for 'velvet' and 'hook' ('velour' and 'crochet').

It took a full ten years to come up with the technology to weave the loops and trim the hooks, but in 1951 de Mestral applied for his patent. By 1957 he had set up business in the USA with a factory in New Hampshire, and a year later mention of the 'zipperless zipper' made its way into the newspapers. In its early days Velcro was regarded as a rather unglamorous and utilitarian invention, but it was taken on with enthusiasm by both NASA, who realised its potential to keep things in place in a weightless atmosphere, and the US military, who saw how it might serve them on the battlefield. Over subsequent decades, it found favour with skiers and divers and today it's widely used in fashion and, especially, footwear. Indeed, it's no overstatement to say that the world has become hooked.

Turning a positive into a negative

The camera obscura – in which light from an object or scene is concentrated through a hole in the side of a box to reproduce an upside-down image of the object or scene on a display surface opposite – has probably existed for thousands of years. In the 16th century Leonardo da Vinci famously recorded his extensive experiments with the camera obscura as a means of capturing an image. However, it was only in the 19th century that photography began to develop so that an image could be fixed onto a surface for a long period of time. Louis Jacques Maude Daguerre was the man who made the great breakthrough with his invention, the Daguerrotype. Yet, after many years grafting in the field, it took a cracked thermometer in a cupboard to secure his fame.

Daguerre was born in France in 1787 and made his name as an artist and theatre designer. In the 1820s, Joseph Nicéphore Niépce, a printer by trade, showed the first fixed photograph. He used a technique called heliography, in which glass or metal plates coated in 'bitumen of Judea' were exposed to light, via a camera obscura, to create an image. After the bitumen had hardened, the plate was washed with lavender oil, leaving behind a 'permanent' image. Although it was a massive improvement on any previous attempts to capture a real-life scene, in truth the image was very faint. Daguerre saw the potential, though, and the two men formed a business partnership around 1829.

Niépce died only four years later but Daguerre continued with their work. He developed a system whereby silver-plated copper plates were exposed to iodine vapour, thus producing a coating of silver iodide on the plate. An image was then made using the camera obscura, but the images continued to lack intensity or depth. Daguerre took one of the disappointing plates and put it in a cupboard ready for cleaning and re-use. But when he returned to it a few days later he found that the image had an unfamiliar sharpness.

He realised that the plate must have reacted with a chemical in the cupboard. Unfortunately, the cupboard was full of chemicals, so each day he put one of the photographic plates in and took one of the chemicals out, working on the basis that the image would remain unchanged once the relevant substance was removed. However, he had soon emptied the cupboard of all its chemicals and still the plates showed an intense image. Then he made a closer study of the inside of the cupboard and on one shelf found a few drops of mercury that had spilled from a broken thermometer. That had to be the magic ingredient.

Daguerre kept on experimenting and discovered that the best results came from coating the photographic plate with vapour from mercury heated to 75° Celsius, before permanently fixing the image with a salt solution. It was 1839 and the Daguerreotype was born. Daguerre sold his patent for the process to the French government, providing himself and the son of Niépce with a pension for life. The French government in turn made a gift of the process to the world.

Daguerrotypes were expensive to produce and were eventually superseded by cheaper, quicker methods that also allowed for multiple prints. Nonetheless, they all owe a debt of gratitude to Daguerre and the faulty thermometer that launched the era of modern photography.

The secretary's secret

Bette Nesmith was the inventor of Liquid Paper, a paint-on substance that can be used to erase mistakes on paper. A boon to secretaries all around the globe, the product made Bette a millionaire many times over. A secretary herself, it was the arrival of some painters to tidy up her office windows that inspired her creation.

Born Bette Clair McMurray in Dallas, Texas in 1924, she left school at seventeen to attend secretarial college. By the age of 22 she had married and divorced Warren Nesmith, with whom she had a son, Michael. Confronted with bringing up a child on her own, Bette became a secretary for the Texas Bank & Trust. Her diligence saw her become executive secretary to the chairman of the board, but by her own admission she wasn't the world's most brilliant typist. And with the growing use of the electric typewriter, it was becoming ever harder to hide any typos she might make. Any serious error meant retyping the whole affected page.

While mulling over this problem, Bette spotted a team of decorators turning up at the office to give its windows the once-over. She watched as they corrected any mistake they might make by simply applying another layer of paint, with no one any the wiser. A light bulb went on in her imagination. Something of an amateur artist herself, Bette went home and found some water-based tempera paint, which she put into a bottle and took to work the next day along with a watercolour brush.

She found the paint solution remarkably effective for covering over any mistakes in her work. However, unsure what the reaction of her bosses would be to her creation (and presumably to the fact that she was making mistakes at all), she kept it secret for five years. She used this time to improve the solution, even calling in the help of her son's chemistry teacher, and it wasn't long before other secretaries had cottoned on to her secret weapon and asked for supplies of their own. In 1956 she went into commercial production in her spare time, mixing the initial batches in a kitchen blender. Marketing it as 'Mistake Out', she had modest sales of about 100 bottles a month.

But interest in the new product soon gathered pace. In 1958 it was rebranded 'Liquid Paper' and Bette registered her patent. After apparent misuse of bank stationery, she was fired from her secretarial position in 1958 and devoted herself full-time to 'Liquid Paper'. Within a decade she was selling a million bottles per year, with the product coming in a variety of colours. In 1979, when Gillette Corporation bought Bette out for $47·5 million, her company was producing over 25 million bottles each year. It was a good time to sell, too, as the emergence of the word processor inevitably ate away at demand.

Bette, who had spent several years pursuing philanthropic endeavours, died only a few months later in 1980. Half of her fortune went to her son Michael, who himself had found considerable fame as a member of The Monkees.

A sticky situation

In the era of the paperless office, Post-it Notes have carved themselves a special place in the hearts of all office workers. Whether you're noting down a phone message for a colleague, marking *your* carton of milk in the fridge as *yours*, or – for the more advanced Post-it Noter – using a whole rainbow of hues for a highly intricate colour-coding exercise, they're invaluable.

So it's only right and proper that they should have been invented entirely by accident. Spencer Silver was a research chemist working in the labs of the 3M Company in Minnesota in the late 1960s. He was charged with developing an adhesive that was strong enough to outperform the products already on 3M's books. Things didn't go entirely to plan, and by 1968 Silver found that he had a new sort of glue that stuck to things – but only just. It was, essentially, the opposite of superglue and met very few of his initial goals.

However, he noticed that it would stick papers together which could then be pulled apart undamaged. Sensing that he was on to something, he developed the idea of selling it as a spray to attach papers to white boards or other flat surfaces. The company, though, remained to be convinced. After several years, a fellow 3M worker, Arthur Fry, attended one of Silver's seminars. Fry was a keen chorister who used markers to keep his place in his hymnal. However, he grew frustrated when they kept falling out, so he decided to give Silver's spray a go. He found that it kept the bookmarks just so, and they could then be removed without ripping his hymn book.

Fry presented his bosses with a prototype sticky bookmark that, after initial scepticism, soon won round his fellow workers. An initial launch in 1977 stumbled but, after an overwhelming response to a run of free samples, Post-its were relaunched onto an unsuspecting US market in 1980. By 1998 estimated worldwide sales stood at US$1 billion. It's to Silver and Fry's credit that they had much greater sticking power than their invention.

CHAPTER 2

Today's Specials

No chef who ever cut the mustard has gone without the odd culinary disaster. Mixing up your sugar and your salt, forgetting to put in the eggs, or setting your oven to Centigrade rather than Fahrenheit usually results in a plate of something inedible and a lesson well learned. Every now and then, though, a mishap in the kitchen can lead to the discovery of a lifetime.

I want to teach the world to drink

Dr John Pemberton was a pharmacist from Atlanta, Georgia with a penchant for creating new potions and remedies. There was his French Wine Coca (a subtle concoction of wine and cocaine) to relieve those with ailing nerves, while for his customers embarrassed by greying hair he offered hope in the form of Pemberton's Indian Queen Magic Hair Dye.

When the spectre of Prohibition loomed into view in Atlanta in 1886, Pemberton started working on a non-alcoholic version of his Wine Coca. Stirring his secret mixture in a kettle with a boat oar, he came up with a new syrup that he claimed could cure an assortment of ills, including headaches and exhaustion. He took it to the local Jacob's Pharmacy for the proprietor to test and he was impressed.

However, it took Pemberton's erstwhile associate, Willis Venable, to succumb to a lapse of concentration for 'the world's favourite drink' to come into existence. Venable accidentally mixed a batch using carbonated, rather than still, water. The reaction of those who tasted it was one of overwhelming enthusiasm. The product was rebranded Coca-Cola (reflecting the use of cocaine and cola nuts in its original preparation) and it was sold not as a medicine but as a restorative soda fountain drink. Jacob's charged 5 cents a glass.

Nonetheless, Pemberton wasn't to enjoy the full benefits of his serendipitous creation. First-year sales were modest, at just under ten glasses per day. When his marketing costs were taken into account, Pemberton made a loss of about $25 for the year. The following year he sold the rights to his drink to Asa Griggs Candler, whose initial investment of $2,300 saw him eventually rake in millions. By 2008 the Coca-Cola Company was operating in over 300 territories around the world and it was estimated that over 1½ billion servings of its various brands were dispensed each day.

Bag to the future

The preparation of tea has been a celebrated art for many centuries, with different areas of the world developing their own distinct customs and techniques. But as the 20th century dawned, there was a problem. Tea was no longer the preserve of the rich, who could afford to employ domestic staff to oversee the time-consuming process needed to produce a really good brew. It was now the drink of the people, and people wanted a cuppa in a hurry.

By chance, around this time a New York tea and coffee trader by the name of Thomas Sullivan was trying to figure out how he could cut his business costs. He was in the habit of sending samples to his various customers in cans that were expensive both to produce and to ship. In an inspired moment of penny pinching, he chose instead to pack the loose tea leaves into small, hand-sewn silk parcels.

A number of devices had already been invented for the optimum diffusion of tea, usually consisting of a perforated metal container which was filled with leaves and dunked into boiling water for the desired period of time. With these no doubt in mind, several potential customers of Sullivan believed the bags were a variation on the theme and didn't bother to decant the leaves from their silk container, but plonked the whole thing in the cup. Soon the orders came rolling in, not simply for his tea but for the bags it came in too. There were even suggestions as to how he might improve the design.

Sullivan developed his prototype, experimenting with gauze mesh and then paper, as well as varying the size of the bags so that they could cater either for a cup or a full pot. He also included a string attachment for easy extraction from the water. The developmental zenith came in 1930 when

William Hermanson, an employee at the Boston-based Technical Papers Corporation, perfected the heat-sealed paper fibre teabag.

The American market was won over to the idea of the teabag almost immediately. The British, though, took longer to convince. Tea was simply not something to be dabbled with. Yet Tetley introduced them to the market in the 1950s and, after some hesitancy, they took hold. Today, something like 96 per cent of all cuppas are made with bags.

The hole truth

The doughnut – essentially a fried cake – is never going to be able to boast the highest health credentials. There's but one way to make a solid slab of deep-fried dough slightly less terrible for your arteries, and that's to eat less of it. In this respect, the ring doughnut with its hole in the middle can be the only choice for the health-conscious.

The ring doughnut owes its creation to Hanson Gregory, a sailor born in the American state of Maine in 1832. His invention came not from any deep concern for an expanding waistline but, if legend is to be believed, was the result of his search for a pragmatic solution to a problem peculiar to the sea-going man.

The story goes that Gregory was just about to tuck into his favourite food one stormy evening on the ocean wave. But before he had a chance to sample his doughnut, the wind blew up fiercely and Gregory was forced to turn his attentions to the welfare of the ship. With a gale now blowing, the vessel was fighting hard against Gregory, and it took all of his strength just to keep it going in the right direction. With both hands firmly needed on the ship's wheel, he was faced with a dilemma: what was he to do with his supper? He was decisive in his actions, sticking it over one of the wheel's wooden spokes, so that the doughnut centre was pushed out.

When the storm had calmed and he was able to sit down and quietly enjoy his sweet treat, he realised that the overall experience was enhanced by the loss of the doughnut centre. All too often this was the bit of the cake that had a slightly soggy, unpleasant texture. From that moment on, he requested that the ship's cook continue to prepare his doughnuts with holes in the middle.

Corn of plenty

Cornflakes have been the favoured breakfast of millions for decades, and paved the way for the multi-billion-dollar breakfast cereal industry. They were invented – perhaps discovered is a better word – by the Kellogg brothers who ran a sanatorium in Michigan, where culinary invention was very low on the agenda.

Of the two brothers, the elder, John Harvey (J. H.), was by far the more serious; while the younger, Will Keith (W.K.), was blessed with a fierce entrepreneurial streak. Raised as devout Seventh-Day Adventists in Battle Creek, Michigan, the boys were taught from a young age about the benefits of a healthy lifestyle. In 1875, J.H. qualified as a doctor and took over the running of the Health Reform Institute in Battle Creek, remodelling it as a 'Sanitarium' to spread his health reform ideas. His key to well-being lay in good diet, exercise, rest and fresh air – an approach that he was convinced kept both body and spirit pure and the baser urges under control. With W.K. as the Institute's business manager, Battle Creek won a national reputation.

The Kelloggs' regime called for patients to cut out meat, caffeine, alcohol and tobacco. In a bid to keep interesting what might have been a rather dull menu, the boys invented a few dishes of their own. These included one that was essentially baked sheets of dough, created by putting wheat through rollers before cooking. On a particular day in 1894, a tin of wheat was left out overnight. When it was discovered the next day, the wheat had gone stale but, presumably thinking 'waste not want not', they attempted to put it through the rollers nonetheless. Out came not doughy sheets but thin flakes. They proceeded to toast them and discovered that they were really quite agreeable. Then they exposed some corn to the same treatment and found that it worked even better.

While J.H. was happy enough keeping his discovery in-house, W.K. saw greater potential. However, one patient at the sanatorium, C.W. Post, beat him to the punch, stealing the idea and marketing it through his company, Post Cereal (later General Foods). But all was not lost. W.K. dabbled with the recipe (falling out with his brother over the addition of sugar) and in 1906 established the Battle Creek Toasted Corn Flake Company.

The product was a huge hit, making W.K. a millionaire many times over. The relationship with his brother had been irreparably damaged, though. If proof were needed of the advantages of the Kellogg way of life, both J.H. and W.K. lived to the age of 91.

How maple became a staple

Of North America's many contributions to world culture, few are more appetising than a big pile of pancakes drenched in maple syrup. Canada is the centre of the maple syrup-producing industry, accounting for over 80 per cent of the world's supply. Indeed, the maple leaf has become the country's national symbol, while several US states, including Vermont, are also significant producers. Legend has it that this sweet delight was discovered by chance by an Iroquois chief.

In the early 17th century, so the story goes, there was a chief called Woksis who would get up each day and set off hunting along with his trusty companion, a tomahawk. One March evening on returning home (perhaps after a bad day at the office) he flung his tomahawk away and it embedded itself in the trunk of a maple tree.

When Woksis left to go hunting the following day, he wrenched the tomahawk from the tree. At the foot of the maple was a bucket which the chief's family filled every day with water from the local river. March, we now know, is the peak of the maple syrup season, when a combination of icy cold nights and warm days promotes the flow of sap. So when Woksis' wife went to get the bucket later in the morning, she saw that it was filled with a liquid that had flowed from the gash in the tree's bark. Rather than go to the river, she decided she would use this sap for the day's cooking.

When dinner was served that evening, everyone was delighted by the sweetness of the food which had absorbed the flavours of the syrup produced as the sap boiled down. Various Native American tribes began to harvest the sap, using tomahawks to carve V-shaped incisions into the trunks of maples and then directing the secretions into buckets. It was only a matter of time before the taste buds of European settlers were tickled too and maple syrup established itself as a global commodity. Its popularity was further assured when, during the American Civil War, abolitionists adopted it in favour of sugar cane produced by the slaves of the Southern states.

Ice on the prize

The creator of the ice lolly, the perfect treat on a hot day, was an eleven-year-old boy who absent-mindedly left a drink out on a cold night. Mulling over his accidental creation for almost twenty years, it eventually made him a very rich man.

In 1905 Frank Epperson was a regular kid growing up in San Francisco. One evening he was mixing himself a drink of water and soda water powder, which he stirred with a wooden stick. Something then distracted his attention and he forgot all about his drink, which was left on the back porch for what turned out to be a particularly cold night. When Frank returned to it the next morning, he found that the liquid had frozen solid. He ran the glass under the hot tap and removed the flavoured ice, with the end of the wooden stirrer a perfect handle. He was delighted with his refreshing fruity icicle. Frank was without doubt the coolest kid in town that day.

Frank called his invention an 'Epsicle', but it would be seventeen years before the public got a first taste of them when they were served up at a ball game in Oakland. The following year Frank applied for a patent and set up a company to sell his Epsicles. Fortunately for him, Frank had children of his own by now, and they weren't impressed with the name, persuading him that 'Popsicle' was far better. Initially available in seven flavours, Frank's Popsicles were an immediate hit. With the growing popularity of home freezers in the 1950s, sales received another boost. In North America at least, Popsicle became the generic name for all ice lollies on a stick. Today they come in 30 flavours (though it's classic orange that remains the favourite) and sell in excess of a billion a year.

The thin end of the (potato) wedge

The world's favourite snack, the potato crisp, was invented in the mid-19th century in New York by the head chef of an upmarket restaurant who succumbed to a fit of temper.

George Speck was born in Saratoga Lake, New York, in 1822. His mother was a Native American from the Huron tribe, while his father was an African-American jockey who raced under the name 'Crum'. George was to adopt this as his own surname.

George was a talented chef and found work in one of Saratoga Springs' most esteemed eateries, the Moon Lake Lodge resort. Its menu included French-fried potatoes, a dish made popular in the late 18th century by Thomas Jefferson, who had got a taste for the deep-fried chips when serving as ambassador to France.

On 24 August 1853 the restaurant hosted a particularly spiky diner who returned his chips to the kitchen, where George was working with his sister Kate, and asked that they should be cut thinner. George produced another plate that were again returned. Flying into a rage characteristic of so many great chefs, George took the diner's demands to their extreme. He sliced the potatoes into wafer-thin pieces and fried the life out of them until he had a plate full of brown, crunchy potato crisps.

Possibly to George's chagrin, the diner was delighted with them and had soon persuaded his fellow diners that they were missing out. 'Saratoga Chips' were soon a regular feature of the Moon Lake Lodge menu and in time they were served in a basket on every table as the restaurant's signature dish.

His name made, George opened his own restaurant, 'Crumbs House', in 1860 and for the next 30 years made a very nice living for himself. Crucially, though, he never took out a patent on his creation. It was only in 1895 that a local businessman, William Tappendon, started manufacturing crisps for sale in local grocery stores. In 1926 Laura Scudder made the next great breakthrough when she started putting them in sealed bags to retain freshness. Today, sales of crisps in the USA alone are worth more than an annual $6 billion.

Another culinary delight that owes its existence to overworked kitchen staff is Tarte Tatin, essentially an upside-down apple tart. Legend has it that it was created at the Hotel Tatin at Lamotte-Beuvron, France, at the end of the 19th century. Two sisters, Stéphanie and Caroline, ran the hotel, with Stéphanie looking after the catering side of things. One of her specialities was apple pie, which involved preparing the apples by gently heating them with butter and sugar. On one particularly busy day, she left the apples on the heat for too long and they began to caramelise. In a last-ditch bid to save the dish, she decided to use the pie's pastry base as a lid before putting the whole lot into the oven to bake. When it came to serving the pudding, she turned the tart upside down and looked on in wonder as her customers delighted in the new creation. A while later, Louis Vaudable visited the hotel and was so taken with the dessert that he took it back to his own restaurant in Paris, Maxim's, thus securing the tart's lasting fame.

Sweet success

In a world cursed with a sweet tooth and paranoia about its calorie intake, the commercial value of producing low-cal synthetic sweeteners is obvious. Yet it's an industry that has relied heavily on chemists stumbling on suitable products while looking for something else entirely.

The first of the great artificial sweeteners to be discovered was saccharin, which emerged from the laboratory of Ira Remsen at Johns Hopkins University in Baltimore. Born in New York in 1846, Remsen studied extensively in Germany and brought his experiences back to the USA, where he's credited with establishing the first American chemistry lab to rival its European counterparts. In 1879 his lab was undertaking research work on coal tar, including toluene derivatives. Among the researchers was the Russian-born Constantin Fahlberg, who was working on his doctorate. After a hard day in the lab, both men detected an intense sweet taste on their fingers. (Some versions of the tale claim that Remsen noticed this when tucking in to a roll.) Fahlberg seized on the commercial potential of this side-product of their experiments. He developed a method of commercial synthesis and took out a patent for what he called 'saccharin' in 1884. Remsen, though, wasn't happy at being cut out of the equation and the two men would continue to bicker as to who had actually made the discovery. Saccharin grew in popularity during the sugar shortages of the First World War and won even more fans in the latter part of the 20th century as understanding of its low-calorie qualities increased.

The next big discovery was made in 1937 by a 25-year-old chemist of Czech extraction, Dr Michael Sveda. He was studying for his doctorate at the University of Illinois, looking at the properties of a group of compounds called sulfamates. When he started to smoke a cigarette without having washed his hands, he picked up a sweet taste on his lips which he traced back to the sodium cyclohexylsulfamate he had been working with. He continued to experiment with the substance while an employee of the DuPont Company and took out a patent in 1939. The non-caloric sweetener became a serious rival to saccharin and was used in some of the most popular low-cal food and drinks on the market. However, tests on rats suggested that it might have carcinogenic properties and it was banned in 1970. These results have subsequently been much questioned. Sveda remained upbeat, though, and fully acknowledged the role of providence in his discovery, commenting that: 'God looks after damn fools, children and chemists.'

The third discovery, of aspartame (sold under trade names including NutraSweet and Candarel) came in 1965 when Jim Schlatter, a chemist with the G.D. Searle company, was attempting to synthesise a tetrapeptide (a combination of four amino acids) for the purpose of testing an anti-ulcer drug. In the course of this work, he made a substance called aspartyl-phenylalanine methyl ester. As he heated the substance, some found its way onto the outside of a flask and was transferred to Schlatter's fingers. When he later went to pick up a piece of paper, he licked his finger and was struck by the deep sweetness in his mouth. Confident that the substance was non-toxic, he and a lab partner put a little in some coffee and tasted it. His boss at Searle, Dr Bob Mazur, knew they had stumbled onto a winning formula. With a sweetness roughly 180 times greater than that of sugar, by the mid-1980s aspartame was generating over $1 billion per year.

Using your loaf

Appropriately for a beverage so associated with confusion and memory loss, the origins of beer are somewhat hazy. However, all the available evidence suggests that beer was discovered quite by chance by the Sumerians, one of the great civilisations of the ancient world.

The Sumerian civilisation was located in the area broadly covered by modern-day southern Iraq and which has come to be known as the 'cradle of civilisation'. The Sumerians were among the first humans to give up on the nomadic life-style in favour of farming around permanent settlements.

They were soon able to harvest grain on a regular basis and, perhaps as a way of preserving it, they would bake it into an early form of bread which they then stored. Some time around 6,000 years ago, a batch of this bread somehow became wet and within a short time had begun to ferment. Soon the bread started to ooze a strange pulp that ancient records suggest left those brave enough to try it feeling 'exhilarated, wonderful and blissful'.

Realising that they had stumbled onto something with the potential to change the world (or at least the consumer's perception of it), the brewing industry began in earnest – though it was very much the preserve of women. It would seem that some bread was baked with the express purpose of adding it to water to form a liquidy mash that was left to ferment. Drinking straws were even invented for the purpose of extracting the bitter ale from the gunky pulp. To sweeten the flavour, honey or fruit was added.

As many modern drinkers believe beer to be the nectar of the gods, the Sumerians had their own goddess of beer and brewing called Ninkasi. She was the subject of a hymn written around 1800 BC that represents perhaps the earliest written recipe for beer-makers. It concludes by likening the opening of a cask of filtered ale to 'the onrush of the Tigris and Euphrates'. A romantic image indeed, and one to hold on to next time you awake after a big night out with a cracking headache and the suspicion that a badger has been sleeping in your mouth.

CHAPTER 3

Great Leaps Forward

It can be strange to think that some of the truly great progressions in human development came laced with a liberal coating of pure, unbidden good luck. Yet some of the finest minds and most intrepid and creative spirits of our species have needed a bit of unprompted fortune on the way to realising their greatest achievements. Indeed, William Shakespeare, himself no slouch in terms of human accomplishment, recognised just this situation. In *Cymbeline* he noted that 'Fortune brings in some boats that are not steered'. Just ask Christopher Columbus ...

Lost and found

Christopher Columbus is 'the man who discovered America', the founder of the 'New World' who was in fact only hoping to find a new route to Asia. Without him, it may be argued, European colonisation of both South and North America might have been delayed by decades, even centuries, and the history of the modern world might have spiralled off in a quite different direction. So it was that the fate of humanity was subject to the whim of Columbus and a robustly inaccurate piece of navigation. A powerful thought to consider next time you're struggling to find a turn-off in your *A–Z*.

Columbus was born in Genoa in 1451 and took to the sea when a teenager. He then settled in Portugal, where he formulated a scheme to chart a westward route to Asia via the Atlantic Ocean. His idea was rooted in two misconceptions – that there was a clear stretch of water between Europe and Asia, and that the earth has a significantly smaller diameter than is actually the case. These misconceptions were the result of his reliance on a globe, considered the most accurate of the day, designed by Martin Behaim. It was alas based on a global circumference calculated by Ptolemy in the early 2nd century AD that underestimated the planet's size by about a quarter.

Columbus spent several years trying to find backing for his great voyage but was turned down by Portugal, France, England and the city states of Genoa and Venice. Then in the early 1490s he tried out his plan on Spain's Queen Isabella. With the traditional overland routes to Asia increasingly precarious, he eventually persuaded her to finance his ambitious trip.

Columbus set off on 3 August 1492, captaining his legendary fleet of three ships: *Santa María*, *Pinta* and *Niña*. In October, ten weeks later, and just as his disillusioned crew were on the point of mutiny, he spied land. It was an island that Columbus named San Salvador but which would become part of the Bahamas. He went on to explore the north-east coast of Cuba and the island of Hispaniola, and established a settlement on what has become Haiti before setting off on the return trip to Spain. It was the first of four voyages that Columbus would lead to the New World.

On the second voyage, in 1493, he was accompanied by 1,200 men intent on colonisation of these new lands. The third and fourth trips, in 1498 and 1502, saw Columbus, as Governor of the Indies, dealing with uprisings from native peoples and discontent among the colonisers. Columbus took a hard line and even faced trial in Spain for the brutality of his rule before being freed by royal decree.

For a great deal of his remaining years he stubbornly held that he had uncovered new Asian lands, despite other explorers and colonists being quite clear that these lands formed a distinct new territory. Columbus died, famous and wealthy, in Valladolid in 1506.

Whether or not he himself accepted the fact, Columbus was responsible for introducing Europe to the Americas and so brought together those two worlds. He paved the way for the exchange of people, goods, cultures and philosophies that have marked the world ever since. His legacy is, of course, not wholly untainted, for the intercontinental exchange included the introduction of crushing diseases, the establishment of a brutal slave trade and the European oppression of the native people of the Americas. But for good and bad, our global history was moulded by his miscalculated path to Asia.

It's interesting to note that Leif Ericsson, almost certainly the first European to set foot in North America, arrived nearly 500 years ahead of Columbus after hearing of another sailor's chance encounter with the new land. According to the Icelandic Sagas, Ericsson headed west from Greenland on the basis of the claims of an Icelandic trader, Bjarni Herjulfsson. Herjulfsson had seen, though not visited, a huge new land-mass after a great storm had blown his vessel massively off course. Retracing his steps, Ericsson came upon what were probably the coasts of Newfoundland and Labrador. Unlike Columbus' great voyages, though, Ericsson's trip didn't end in colonisation, and a long-term relationship between the continents was left to others to forge.

Bathed in glory

Archimedes was a master of many disciplines, furthering human knowledge of maths, physics and astronomy as well as employing his engineering skills to come up with many practical inventions. Perhaps the most famous of all his mathematical theorems is that which explains how the volume of an irregular solid might be calculated by submerging it in water. This knowledge came to him out of the blue as he took a restful dip in the bath.

Although information on Archimedes' life is patchy, we do know that he was born in Syracuse in Sicily (then part of Magna Graecia) around 287 BC. Among his myriad achievements, he explained the principles of levers, gave a very accurate estimation of Pi, made huge advances in hydro-statics and proved that the volume of a sphere is two-thirds that of the cylinder in which it is inscribed. The latter he considered to be his crowning achievement. It's also likely that he invented the screw that now bears his name (an early means of pumping water), as well as an assortment of weapons and siege machines.

It was the Roman writer Vitruvius who explained how Archimedes came up with his new method of measuring volume during the course of his ablutions. King Hiero II of Syracuse had commissioned a golden crown in the form of a laurel wreath. Clearly having little trust in his goldsmith, he wanted to be sure that the gold content hadn't been diluted by the use of lesser metals. So it was essential that he knew how much the crown weighed and what its volume was. A simple calculation could then be made to discover its density, which could be compared against the known density of gold. Archimedes was brought in to solve the problem, along with a warning that the crown could in no way be damaged.

He was pondering the conundrum while having a bath one day. It was then that he noticed how the water level rose when he got in and would fall when he got out. Water being an incompressible substance, he realised that the amount of water displaced must be equal to the volume of the object that displaced it – and so submerging the king's crown in water would allow its volume to be known. Overjoyed with this flash of inspiration, he went on a flash of his own, reputedly running naked through the streets shouting 'Eureka!' ('I have found it!').

Archimedes' love of mathematics would tragically cost him his life. Syracuse was captured by Roman forces during the Second Punic War in 212 BC. Special orders had been given that Archimedes should be captured but not killed. His knowledge was too valuable for that. According to Plutarch, when troops were sent to summon him to General Marcellus, he refused to go until he had finished working on a particular problem. An outraged soldier then killed him with his sword.

The tree of knowledge

Isaac Newton, one of the great figures of science, was born in 1642, a short while after the death of Galileo, who had altered humanity's view of the world by proving that the sun was at the centre of the planetary system and not the earth.

His brain filled with such revolutionary ideas, it was unlikely that Newton would ever be content to tend the family farm in Lincolnshire, and so it proved when he took himself off to study at Cambridge. Legend then has it that sometime during the mid-1660s Newton was sitting in the shade of a tree when an apple fell, bumped him on the head and set in motion the thought process that would culminate in his greatest achievement: the Law of Universal Gravitation.

This law states that the force between any two bodies is directly proportional to the product of their masses and inversely proportional to the square of the distance between them. The constant of proportionality is called the gravitational constant. Or to put it more simply, what goes up must come down. Published in his great work, *Principia Mathematica*, in 1687 (which also included his three laws of motion), his ideas had an immediate impact. Not least, they explained how the moon kept turning round the earth without crashing.

In truth, the 'fruit–bonce collision' has little basis in historical fact, but Newton himself confirmed that his theory began to form on watching an apple plummet from a tree to the ground. Something, he reasoned, was pulling it down. And the same something worked no matter how tall the tree was. Perhaps this unknown force extended even beyond the limits of the earth.

There are several candidates for the location of this fateful tree. The garden of Woolsthorpe Manor, the Newton family home, has a strong claim, though a local school has suggested that the tree was uprooted and relocated to its grounds. Trinity College, Cambridge – Newton's old college – also boasts a descendant from the original.

Plotting the future

René Descartes was a man of big ideas, often regarded as the founder of modern philosophy for his questioning of all previous systems of thought and knowledge, highlighting the fallibility of human perception and insisting on deduction as the only valid method of investigation. His most famous principle is summed up by the memorable 'Cogito ergo sum' ('I think, therefore I am') – essentially, an assertion that the only things we can be certain of are the existence of thought and of the thinking individual. Much of Descartes' work was of a more practical nature, though, and he made great contributions to the study of mathematics and the natural sciences. One of his most important legacies was the rectangular coordinate system, more commonly known as Cartesian coordinates. It's perhaps reassuring to the rest of us that this breakthrough resulted from Descartes lounging around in bed and staring at the wall.

Cartesian coordinates allow us to create graphs to indicate different points in two- or three-dimensional spaces. To render points on a two-dimensional surface, the graph is created by marking the points against two calibrated perpendicular lines (the x-axis and the y-axis). A third z-axis is added for points in three-dimensional space. In this way geometric shapes can be represented by algebraic equations. The system provided the basis for analytical geometry and calculus, and its many applications have been essential to mathematicians, physicists, cartographers, economists and technologists ever since.

Descartes was born in France in 1596, in the town of La Haye en Touraine (which was subsequently renamed Descartes). He initially trained as a lawyer but moved to the Netherlands where he would carry out much of his greatest mathematical and philosophical work. His theories on

Cartesian coordinates were published in 1637 in *La Géométrie*, part of his wider work *Discours de la méthode* (*Discourse on the Method*).

In his childhood Descartes had attended a Jesuit school where, dogged by ill health, he had grown accustomed to spending his mornings meditating in bed. He would remain a late riser all his life, rarely starting his practical work before midday. So it was that one morning he was reclining in his room when he became distracted by a fly. He followed its path as it buzzed around from one spot on the bedroom wall to another. Using the 'axes' created at the corner of the room where the walls and ceiling met, he realised he could describe the fly's location at any given moment in relation to them. The Cartesian coordinate system was born.

Several years later, Queen Christina of Sweden persuaded Descartes to come and teach her in Stockholm. It was there that he died in 1650 from pneumonia, some believing that it was Christina's demand for early morning lessons that did for him.

An explosive legacy

The name of Alfred Nobel, the 19th-century Swedish chemist and engineer, is synonymous with one of mankind's most destructive inventions, dynamite, and with a series of prizes celebrating the peaks of human achievement. Both owe much to the intervention of serendipity.

Nobel was born in Stockholm in 1833 and moved with

his family to St Petersburg in Russia when he was nine. There his father, Immanuel, worked in developing military explosives, prospering until the end of the Crimean War saw him lose everything. The Nobels returned to Sweden in 1861 and Alfred joined his father in setting up a factory in Stockholm to produce nitroglycerine, a liquid explosive that had been invented by an Italian, Ascanio Sobrero, back in the 1840s. Tragedy awaited the Nobels when, in 1864, a huge explosion at their factory killed five people, including Alfred's younger brother, Emil. The accident also caused Immanuel to have a stroke, leaving Alfred responsible for the family's welfare.

With the wound of his brother's death still raw, Alfred set out to develop a process by which nitroglycerine could be made more stable and safer to manufacture. He attempted to add the substance to a range of materials including methyl alcohol, sawdust, paper and charcoal to reduce the chance of accidental explosion, but none of these methods was very satisfactory.

Then one day Nobel discovered that one of his cans of nitroglycerine had sprung a leak. The can was packed with several others, each separated by a quantity of kieselguhr, a lightweight porous mineral native to Germany. Nobel saw how the liquid had soaked into it and the cogs of his mind began to whirr. He discovered that the nitroglycerine-imbued kieselguhr could be moulded into a putty-like compact solid, retaining its explosive potential but needing a blasting cap to set it off. He had created dynamite, a substance that could be used for large-scale demolition in building projects and, of course, in weaponry. It was one of 155 patents that Nobel secured during his life, and would make him a personal fortune.

The second great moment of serendipity came later in Alfred's life. In 1888 his brother Ludvig died. A French newspaper mixed the brothers up and erroneously printed Alfred's obituary under the title 'The merchant of death is dead'. Alfred was dismayed to think that he would be remembered in such terms, and set his mind to leaving some lasting good. In 1895 he signed his last will and testament, bequeathing 31 million kronor to fund a series of prizes to be awarded annually to the person or persons (regardless of nationality) who have made what the administrating committee believe to be the greatest contribution in the fields of Physics, Chemistry, Medicine, Literature and Peace. The Nobel Prizes today are arguably the most admired awards in the world.

Out of this world

It's perhaps a blessing that Clyde Tombaugh, the man who discovered Pluto in 1930, didn't live to see 2006, when the subject of his greatest work was downgraded from a planet to a dwarf planet. Dwarf or not, for the duration of the 20th century Pluto was the ninth planet in our solar system and its discovery was one of the landmark events for astronomers of the period.

Tombaugh was only 24 when he tracked Pluto, and it was the result of impressive and exacting work over the course of several months. His young man's eyes also proved essential. But were it not for some rather wayward assumptions of the long-dead founder of the laboratory at which he studied, it's unlikely that Tombaugh would ever have had the chance to find his extraterrestrial gem.

Percival Lowell was born in 1855 and was a successful businessman with a keen, if eccentric, interest in astronomy. He was particularly well known for claiming that there were identifiable canals on the surface of Mars. His theory gave weight to the argument that the planet might sustain intelligent life. In order to further his studies, Lowell established an observatory amid the mountains at Flagstaff in Arizona.

From his studies there of the solar system, Lowell claimed that he could detect a slight wobble in the orbit of the planet Uranus. This he put down to it being affected by an as yet unknown celestial body, a hypothetical 'Planet X'. He and his team made extensive calculations in a bid to identify the exact location of the celestial body, but by the time of Lowell's death in 1916 the planet remained undiscovered.

Tombaugh won a post at the Lowell Observatory in 1929. He was charged with inspecting photographs of the sky taken every few nights in search of potential planetary movement. Each image contained between 200,000 and 300,000 objects, yet, in a remarkable feat of detection, it took Tombaugh less than a year to spot a tiny speck that seemed to be on the move. That speck turned out to be Pluto. Tombaugh and the observatory won worldwide acclaim.

It also seemed to vindicate Lowell's much derided theory. But the reality was that Lowell had been quite wrong. Uranus' wobble was just an illusion and Pluto certainly played no role in its orbit. It was thus only a piece of intergalactic good luck that saw him misconstrue the evidence to so precisely predict the potential location of a new planet, within 6° of accuracy.

Starry-eyed

Jocelyn Bell, a young astronomer at Cambridge University in the 1960s, was meant to be engaged in work on quasars, distant celestial objects that emit huge amounts of energy thought to be in part derived from black holes. In fact, she ended up discovering a previously unknown type of star called a pulsar.

Jocelyn Bell was born in 1943 in Belfast. Her father was an architect, and it was a visit to one of his commissions, the Armagh Observatory, that began Jocelyn's fascination with the heavens. She graduated in Physics from the University of Glasgow in 1965 before beginning her PhD in radio astronomy at Cambridge. Radio astronomers look at celestial bodies via the sound waves they emit, allowing for the study of objects that might not be visible with traditional optical telescopes.

Bell was working at Cambridge under Anthony Hewish. She was set to work on constructing a huge radio telescope with which to try to track quasars. The telescope when completed covered an area of 4½ acres and consisted of thousands of antennae connected by over 120 miles of wire. The physical labour involved in building it was considerable, and it's unlikely that Bell had such arduous work in mind when she made her original application to the university.

The telescope was ready by July 1967 and Bell was put in charge of studying the charts of sound waves it produced (eating up around 100 yards of paper a day). The trick was to separate those waves resulting from man's activities on earth from those signals emanating from space and then work out which of the latter suggested something of interest.

In October, she picked up on what she would describe as a 'patch of scruff' on the charts, a pulse coming regularly every 1⅓ seconds. No celestial body had ever been found that sent out signals so rapidly and regularly, so Hewish was convinced it must be coming from a man-made source. But Bell measured the time that the signals were detectable over several nights and found that they corresponded to the astronomical day, which is about four minutes shorter than our own. The pulse was definitely coming from space. She later worked out that the source was some 212 light years away. Within a few months she found three more of these pulsating heavenly bodies, which a journalist called 'pulsars', a name that stuck. Eventually, it was understood that a pulsar was a special type of neutron star (see next entry) that emits a radio wave as it spins. At only 24, Bell had discovered a completely new type of star and propelled forward our understanding of the mysteries of the skies.

However, Bell's tale isn't entirely happy, as she was over-looked for a share of the 1974 Nobel Prize for Physics, which went to Hewish and his colleague, Martin Ryle. Bell, the suggestion seemed to be, had served as little more than a data collector. Thankfully, the wider scientific community has subsequently acknowledged her pivotal role in the discovery.

Ironically, in the early 1990s a Polish-born radio astronomer called Alex Wolszczan was looking for pulsars at the Arecibo Observatory in Puerto Rico when he stumbled upon the first identified planet outside our own solar system. He found a pulsar (snappily titled PSR 1257+12) that span at 161 times a second. It was, however, slightly irregular in its rotations. The reason, he realised, was that at least two planets were exerting gravitational force upon it. In search of quasars, Bell found pulsars; in search of pulsars, Wolszczan found the first extrasolar planet.

Shooting stars

On 9 January 2008 the birth of a supernova was captured on film for the first time. A supernova is a stellar explosion signalling the death of a star. The result is a huge expulsion of energy as a star ejects most of its mass at up to 70 per cent of the speed of light, creating a radiation burst that can illuminate a whole galaxy before fading away. What's left is a neutron star, or a black hole. Supernovae occur perhaps twice a century in any given galaxy. When supernova SN 2008D happened 90 million light years away in a spiral galaxy called NGC 2770, it just so happened that a camera on the NASA Swift satellite was pointing in the right direction.

The oldest recorded supernova, designated SN 185, was documented by astronomers in China in 185 AD. The 2008 Swift satellite was studying a two-week-old supernova in the galaxy NGC 2770, the next best thing to seeing the explosion itself. Most scientists believed the chances of ever capturing such an event were unlikely in the extreme.

For 40 years it had been thought, though never conclusively proved, that as a star dies, a shockwave emits an intense burst of X-rays through its surface. So when Swift detected such a burst lasting five minutes, there was little doubt that a star had just exploded. The team contacted eight other orbiting and ground-based telescopes to make sure the event was caught in as much detail as possible. So it was that SN 2008D was detected, the aftermath of a star that had been about the same size as the sun but roughly 30 times as heavy.

The implications of the discovery are immense for understanding the properties of massive stars, the birth of neutron stars and black holes, and how supernovae impact on their environments. Alicia Sonderberg of the Carnegie Institution and Princeton University acknowledged the role of luck in the discovery: 'We were in the right place, at the right time, with the right telescope on January 9, and witnessed history.'

CHAPTER 4

Uncovering the Past

Most historians and archaeologists have lifetimes of diligent effort rewarded with no particular discoveries of note. Some people, though, trip over finds that provide us with a whole new glimpse at our past and, on occasion, completely change our understanding of who we are and where we come from. Most galling for the unfulfilled antiquarian is the knowledge that, quite often, the finest discoveries are made by those who have no idea of what it is they have found. But as the old saying goes, 'Good luck is often with the man who doesn't include it in his plans.'

All Greek to me

Hieroglyphs was the complex formal writing system used in Egypt at least as early as the 32nd century BC. By the end of the 4th century AD, by which time the invading Romans had seen the closure of all non-Christian temples, it had virtually disappeared. Within generations, those who held the secrets to understanding the language had died too. The rediscovery of these secrets would have to wait almost 1,400 years, when the key to the language was uncovered by chance by Napoleonic forces preparing to do battle with the British.

In the 1790s the French army, led by Napoleon Bonaparte, decided that they could defeat the British in Egypt by wresting control of the rich food supply along the banks of the Nile. Napoleon's forces looked to build a series of forts by making use of the stonework left behind from earlier constructions. In 1799 a group of soldiers were rebuilding and extending a fort near a small village in the Nile Delta called el-Rashid (Rosetta). There a young officer by the name of Pierre-François Bouchard dug up a large chunk of black basalt stone, measuring nearly four feet long, 2½ feet wide and a foot thick. It would come to be known as the Rosetta Stone.

The Rosetta Stone was carved in 196 BC and its inscription is a decree by priests honouring the boy Pharaoh, Ptolemy V. Crucially, the inscription appears in three scripts: Greek (the language of Egypt's ruling class of the time), demotic (the common script of the country), and hieroglyphs (the language of 'officialdom'). It was the first object to be discovered that showed hieroglyphs alongside a comprehensible translation.

Under the terms of the 1801 Treaty of Alexandria, the stone came under British ownership. One Reverend Stephen Weston had completed a comprehensive translation of the Greek text by the following year. Then Thomas Young, an English physicist, and Silvestre de Sacy, a French scholar, managed to make some links between particular words and sounds and their corresponding hieroglyphs. But it was another French academic, Jean-François Champollion, who carried out the bulk of the work that laid the foundations for our modern understanding of the language. He published details of the deciphered hieroglyphs in 1822, opening up a vast new world of possibilities for Egyptologists. Rarely have the actions of an occupying army proved so valuable to our understanding of the world.

She sells sea shells

Mary Anning was born into a poor, lower-class family in Lyme Regis, Dorset in 1799. When Mary was just eleven her father, a cabinet-maker, died, leaving the family all but destitute. However, he did bequeath Mary one thing of enduring value: a passion for fossil-hunting. Combining genius with good fortune, she embarked on a career in which her uncanny ability to discover previously unknown species wowed the scientific world. Mary would come to be known as 'the greatest fossilist the world ever knew'.

Mary and her younger brother, Joseph, were the only survivors of ten children born to her parents. When Mary was two, she survived a lightning strike that killed three other people. Her early years were spent accompanying her father in fossil hunts on the Dorset coast. He trained her how to find specimens and how to prepare them for sale to visitors to the beaches. Indeed, such a familiar face was Mary at their stall that she inspired the tongue-twister: 'She sells sea shells on the sea shore.'

When her father died, the small income Mary made from

trading fossils kept the family just about afloat. Then in 1811 came the first stroke of good fortune. Joseph unearthed a skull sticking out from a cliff face. Mary carefully excavated it over the next few months and revealed a complete skeleton of a crocodile-like creature. It was bought by London's Museum of Natural Curiosities and caused a sensation. It was the first complete skeleton of the Ichthyosaurus ('fish-lizard') ever found. And it had been found by a twelve-year-old girl with barely any formal education.

Mary, though, was literate, and educated herself in geology and anatomy. She proceeded to discover more complete Ichthyosaurus skeletons and followed this up in 1821 with the first example of the Plesiosaurus, a long-necked creature known as the 'sea-dragon'. In 1828 she discovered the first Pterodactylus ('flying-dragon') outside Germany, and the following year came an 'unrivalled specimen' of the Squaloraja, a species somewhere between a shark and a ray.

Her ability to discover new species was unprecedented and she became highly respected among the scientific community. This was a miraculous achievement for the time, given her class and gender. In 1837, members of the British Association for the Advancement of Science and the Geological Society of London granted her an annuity. On her death in 1847 the Geological Society acknowledged her passing, despite the fact that it would be another 57 years before it would admit women into its ranks.

Codebreaking by the book

For over a thousand years, countless secrets were kept via substitution codes. That is to say, a message is transliterated into something apparently meaningless by substituting every letter with a different one. For instance, if a code called for each letter in a word to be represented by the preceding one in the alphabet, 'CODE' would be rendered as 'DPEF'. With something like 400 million million million million potential substitution codes available, there was little chance that a codebreaker would be able to stumble on the right method to decipher any particular message.

Then in the 8th century AD, Islamic theologians set about understanding the exact chronology of the revelations as they appear in the Qur'an. They attempted to do this by analysing the frequency of specific words, on the basis that they knew certain words were associated with an earlier period of time while others were known to have evolved at a later date. The scholars looked not only at words, but continued their analysis with individual letters, highlighting how certain letters appeared far more commonly than others.

This fortuitous scrap of knowledge prompted the thinking of Al-Kindi, an Arab polymath and formidable intellect of the 9th century. Among his many achievements, he was the author of *A Manuscript on Deciphering Crypto-graphic Messages*. Building on the research of the theologians, Al-Kindi developed his theory of cryptanalysis. Using frequency analysis, he explained to codebreakers how they should search for the most common letter in a coded message. For instance, we know that in English, 'E' is the most common letter. If in our encrypted text 'Q' appears most often, we can assume that it represents 'E'. Similarly, we know that 'T' is the second most common letter, so we can repeat the procedure with the next most commonly appearing letter in our code.

The system isn't infallible, but it was the first time in a millennium that codebreakers could realistically take on the challenge of what had previously been thought an unbreakable code. It was a great leap forward in the understanding of cryptography, the result of an incidental discovery of religious scholarship.

High on a hill was a lonely goatherd

In 1947 a goatherd was with his animals near some caves close to the settlement of Qumran on the Dead Sea coast in Israel. Stumbling into one of the caves, he discovered some pottery jars containing ancient leather and papyrus scrolls wrapped in linen. He had found the oldest collection of Old Testament manuscripts known to man. Their importance was quickly grasped throughout the world and, 60 years later, they are key influences on Christian and Jewish scholarship.

The story goes that one particular day in 1947 the unwitting Bedouin goatherd (the identity of whom isn't certain but whose name was probably Mazra) found that one of his goats had strayed. Going in search of it, he threw a rock into a cave and was surprised to hear the sound of breaking pottery. He went in to explore and discovered the jars, but had no idea of their remarkable contents. Mazra took three scrolls that eventually found their way to an antiquities dealer in Bethlehem, who realised they might be of some import. Further trips secured many more samples, although it's said that some were lost forever when they were used as kindling to start fires.

Soon the scrolls made their way on to the antiquities market and word reached the international academic community. Three came into the possession of a scholar at the Hebrew University of Jerusalem and four went to the Archbishop of Syria, who sold them (via a classified advert) to a buyer who in turn donated them to the state of Israel. Altogether some 900 documents (running to 39 published volumes) were found in eleven caves in the area between 1947 and 1956, including texts in Aramaic, Greek and Hebrew. They date from the 3rd century BC to 70 AD, and fall into two groups: Biblical and non-Biblical texts. They include extracts from every book of the Old Testament bar the Book of Esther. Before the discovery of the Dead Sea Scrolls, the oldest known Masoretic (Hebrew) texts dated from the 9th century AD and the oldest Greek texts to the 4th century AD. As might have been predicted, the scrolls have such financial worth and political and religious significance that they have been subject to much controversy concerning ownership, access, authorship and interpretation.

It's not known whether Mazra ever caught up with his errant goat.

Ancient arty facts

The Altamira caves near Santander in northern Spain contain the most impressive collection of Palaeolithic art known to man. They were discovered in the late 19th century by an amateur historian/archaeologist in pursuit of his nine-year-old daughter, who had wandered away from him on a trip to the caves.

The caves had been sealed off for some 13,000 years until they were rediscovered by a local huntsman called Modesto Peres in 1868, when a falling tree dislodged rocks blocking the entrance. The caves were on land owned by Marcelino de Sautuola, a lawyer with a penchant for archaeology. However, it was several years before he was able to devote much time to exploring them, and even then he largely contented himself with studying bone fragments and other artefacts present at the mouth of the caves. In 1879 he paid the site a visit in the company of his daughter, Maria. With almost 300 metres to explore, it was perhaps unsurprising that she careered off on her own. Eventually he caught up with her and, now deep inside the complex, she pointed up to the ceiling which was covered in paintings of bison.

It so happened that Sautuola had visited the World Exposition in Paris the previous year, where he had seen engravings in a similar style. Guessing that the wall paintings might thus date to the Stone Age, he employed the services of Professor Juan Vilanova y Piera, an archaeologist from the University of Madrid. Piera made a study of the paintings, which had been created with charcoal and ochre and included representations not only of bison, but horses, goats, deer and wild boar too. Piera published his findings in 1880, claiming that the artworks dated to the Palaeolithic period. His claims were greeted with delight by the general public but scepticism and ridicule from the academic community. Many doubted the paintings' provenance on the basis of their high quality and excellent state of conservation. Sautuola died in 1888, his caves discredited and largely forgotten.

However, by 1902 other archaeological discoveries, including similar collections of cave paintings in France, confirmed that Piera's hypothesis was entirely accurate. Modern dating analysis puts the artworks at between 11,000 and 19,000 years old.

Nor were these the last ancient cave paintings to be discovered thanks to a child's over-developed sense of adventure. The wonderful animal paintings on the walls of the Lascaux cave in south-west France came to light in 1940 when a gang of four schoolboys found a hole in the ground and decided to crawl inside to explore.

CHAPTER 5

The Big and Small Screens

There are few stars who don't owe their success to a potent blend of talent, dedication and plain old good luck. Some may rightly consider that they have earned every ounce of luck they get in what is a brutally competitive industry. For others, though, the good fortune befalls them in quite unexpected ways. John Barrymore, considered by many the greatest actor of the first half of the 20th century, put it succinctly: 'Happiness often sneaks in through a door you didn't know you left open.'

A toothless performance

Walter Brennan was one of the great character actors in the early days of Hollywood talkies. The first, and indeed only, actor to be awarded three Best Supporting Actor Oscars, Brennan suffered serious facial injuries in a stage fight early in his career. What may have seemed a disaster at the time actually proved to be his making, for it was his 'lived-in' appearance rather than matinee idol good looks that secured him fame and fortune.

Born in 1894 in the town of Swampscott, Massachusetts, Brennan was a keen participant in his school's drama productions. He toured with a musical comedy troop until he joined the army in 1917, serving with the 101st Field Artillery during the First World War. It has been suggested that his distinctive, high-pitched voice that served him so well in the movies was the result of injuries he suffered during a wartime gas attack.

His post-war career was certainly wide-ranging and, according to Brennan himself, included a stint as a pineapple-raiser in Guatemala. He eventually found himself in California, where he made a small fortune in real estate speculation before the bottom fell out of the market.

He had been supplementing his income with a few walk-on roles in films, and in 1923 he began work as a stuntman. By the late 20s he had won a few decent roles in the newly-emerging talkies but it was in 1932 in his capacity as a stuntman that he got his big break, both physically and metaphorically. While taking part in a staged fight, his opposite number was rather over-zealous in his performance, smashing Brennan in the mouth and removing several of his teeth.

With a face that could only be described as 'characterful' and a voice that could have belonged to a man much older than he actually was, Brennan found his services much in demand. On his first day on the set of a new film, Brennan would ask the director, 'With or without?' When the director would respond quizzically, 'With or without what?', Brennan would pop out his dentures and respond: 'Teeth!'

Sam Goldwyn signed him up as a taxi driver in 1935's *The Wedding Night* and liked his performance so much he gave him a long-term contract. Brennan played Swan Bostrom, a Swedish lumberman, in *Come and Get It* the following year, for which he received his first Academy Award. A second followed in 1938 for his performance in *Kentucky*, and a third two years later for *The Westerner*. He was nominated, but didn't win, for *Sergeant York* in 1942. His career never looked back and in the 1950s he conquered television in a number of high-profile series such as *The Real McCoys*. He died in 1974, one of the most respected actors in American screen history.

Tools of the trade

Marlene Dietrich was one of cinema's most enigmatic stars, a woman of simmering sexuality who became a symbol of anti-Nazism and then spent decades as the world's most famous cabaret star. Her big break, though, came as the result of a fortuitous meeting and her mastery of a household tool.

She was born in 1901 as Marie Magdalene Dietrich, a name she would later contract for her career on stage and screen. Brought up in a strict Prussian middle-class family, she was a prodigiously talented violinist who dreamed of a professional career until she catastrophically strained the ligaments in her hand. Her interest then turned to acting and in 1921 she auditioned for Max Reinhardt's famous drama school. However, she was turned down and so joined the chorus of a touring revue show.

During this period she happened to be invited to a party at Reinhardt's home. There her icy beauty was noticed, along with her unexpected talent for playing the saw, a party trick that greatly entertained the other guests. It was 1922 and, a year after being rejected from his school, Reinhardt now invited her to join. It was the spur her career needed.

Marlene made her film debut the following year in *Love Tragedy*. In 1929 she played the lead role of the seductive top hat- and stocking-wearing cabaret singer Lola-Lola in Josef von Sternberg's *The Blue Angel*, the film that made her a legend. In 1930 came an Oscar nomination for *Morocco*.

She worked on six films with von Sternberg and headed up Hollywood box office smashes in the 1930s like *Desire* and *Destry Rides Again*. Hitler's Nazi Germany was keen to reclaim her as one of its own but she refused all approaches, taking American citizenship and speaking out against Hitler's regime. She even travelled to the front line to entertain the American troops, often incorporating her saw into shows.

After the war she focused on her stage rather than screen career, honing her particular blend of sensuality, sophistication, wit and self-effacement in a cabaret that won international acclaim. From the 1970s her public profile diminished as ill health and old age caught up with her, and she spent her last years living in Paris. One would hope she still had the wherewithal to knock out a tune or two on the old saw.

Love in a cold war climate

For 30 years Ronald and Nancy Reagan were one of Hollywood's golden couples. When Ronald became president of the United States in 1980, they became, alongside Prince Charles and Princess Diana, perhaps the most recognisable couple in the world. Yet if it hadn't been for the soaring heat of anti-communist feeling that existed in the USA in the late 1940s, it's quite possible that the Reagans might never have got together.

Nancy was born in 1921 as Anne Frances Robb, but her parents soon divorced and when her mother remarried, Nancy took her stepfather's surname, Davis. It just so happened that there were two Nancy Davises doing the rounds of the Hollywood studios in the second half of the 1940s. So it was with more than a tinge of horror that our Nancy read a newspaper report in Autumn 1949 about the 'Hollywood blacklist' – a register of those suspected of communist (and thus 'anti-American') sympathies. From this article she learned of the inclusion on the list of 'the other Nancy'.

Terrified that producers would confuse the two women, Nancy made contact with the Screen Actors' Guild, which at the time was chaired by ... Ronald Reagan. Reagan agreed to act on Nancy's behalf should her career in any way be affected by the mix-up. Still concerned, she asked for a personal meeting. They duly met on 15 November 1949, promptly fell for each other and were married on 4 March 1952. The rest, as they say, is history.

So it was that Ronald, a man whose personal relationship with the Soviet leader Mikhail Gorbachev helped bring the Cold War to an end, had a little bit of Cold War paranoia to thank for winning him the great love of his life.

One for the road

For much of the world, Indian cinema is Bollywood. However, many critics rate the artful, sensitive and understated films of Satyajit Ray as not only the crowning achievement of Indian cinema but among the gems of world cinema too. Arguably his greatest film was also his first, *Pather Panchali*. It was a misunderstanding over its subject matter that was key to securing the finance to complete it.

Ray was born in Calcutta (now Kolkata) in 1921 and came from a well-respected family, though there was little money to be had during his childhood. He worked in advertising and publishing, where he became noted for his grasp of the power of visual images. In 1947 he co-founded the Calcutta Film Society and five years later began work on what would become his masterpiece.

He took the bold move of funding *Pather Panchali*, a movie about the lives of a boy called Apu and his family in a rural Bengali village, out of his own pocket. He sold some of his own possessions (and indeed some belonging to his wife) to raise finance and employed a cast and crew of mostly amateurs (though many would go on to become stalwarts of the Indian film industry). His hope was that he would get enough good footage to secure backing at a later stage of production. Always an uncompromising artist, he wasn't prepared to negotiate on any aspect of the movie, but he did manage to win the financial support of an American critic who had been suitably impressed by early rushes of the film.

However, the money ran out with a third of the film still left to shoot. Ray turned to the West Bengal authorities for more, and this was his moment of unexpected fortune. *Pather Panchali* translates as *Song of the Little Road*. Amid the over-burdened bureaucracy of the state administration, his funding application somehow found its way to the government's transport division. They appeared to infer from the title that the film was to be a documentary about the state's road network. His application thus succeeded, funds were granted and filming was completed in 1955.

Pather Panchali won immediate critical and popular acclaim and its international impact was ensured with a prize-winning performance at the Cannes Film Festival. Ray went on to complete the *Apu Trilogy* and a host of other landmark pictures. He died in 1992, the same year in which he was awarded an honorary Oscar for his lifetime achievements.

Waiting for inspiration

Sesame Street is an American icon, changing the perception of what children's television could be since it debuted in 1969. Having won well over 100 Emmy awards, its legendary status is in no small part due to Jim Henson's magnificent puppets. Among the most popular of these is Oscar the Grouch, a trash can-dwelling creature who is endearingly loveable despite a rather dour world view – a sort of Eeyore for the Muppet generation. The inspiration for Oscar came in the form of a bad-tempered waiter whose lack of customer service delighted Henson, one of his regular customers.

Oscar greets most of what life throws at him with consistent bad will. Knock on his trash can and you will inevitably be received with a sneer, having no doubt interrupted him from some far more important activity. Annoyance for Oscar is something to be shared, not hidden away. Although there's a softer side to him – he's certainly very fond of Slimey, his pet worm – his greatest joy is to be found in disappointment at the world.

Luckily for Henson, he had at hand a perfect model for Oscar. Henson and a fellow *Sesame Street* director called Jon Stone would often lunch at Oscar's Salt of the Sea, a restaurant in Manhattan, New York. Apparently, many of the original *Sesame Street* designs had their genesis on Oscar's place mats. One of the regular waiters was blessed with a particularly bad attitude and an unerring ability to pop the good mood of diners. His abuse was so unnecessary but reliable that there was a sort of masochistic pleasure to be had in eating there. Indeed, Henson and Stone were able to lift several of the waiter's expressions of disgruntlement and give them straight to Oscar.

A further slice of luck came when Oscar's Muppeteer,

Caroll Spinney, picked up a cab in the Bronx. The driver turned to him and in a gravelly tone muttered, 'Where to, Mac?' First Oscar's character and then his voice were picked up direct from the good citizens of New York. It's a contribution of which the city can be proud. There has been something fundamentally comforting about Oscar's attitude from the moment he spoke his first line: 'Don't bang on my can! Go away.'

Finding the pot of gold

In 2004 the American Film Institute released a list of the 100 best songs to have appeared in American films. At the top was 'Over the Rainbow', performed by the teenaged Judy Garland in the classic 1939 movie, *The Wizard Of Oz*. Yet were it not for a last-minute change of heart by the film's producers, the song would have ended up on the editing room floor.

With music by Harold Arlen and lyrics by E.Y. 'Yip' Harburg, the ballad is a hymn of hope that there's something better to be found 'somewhere over the rainbow'. But it didn't fill director Victor Fleming with great hope for the success of his film when he saw it in preview. Rather, he thought it was an impediment to the flow of the film, 'too long' and 'too difficult'. Fleming was all for cutting it out altogether. Unfortunately for him, phrases from the song were reprised throughout the film and Arlen and executive producer Arthur Freed argued that these phrases would seem strange if Garland's rendition was removed. The two of them persuaded Louis B. Mayer, head of MGM, that the scene had to be kept. Another director then cut the song again, only for Mayer to step in once more.

Mayer's intervention turned out to be fortuitous for all involved. The film was a huge hit, with *that* song its most memorable tune. It won the Oscar for Best Original Song, became the signature tune of Judy Garland throughout her remarkable life, and remains as evocative of innocence and hope today as it ever did.

It wasn't the first time that good fortune had a role to play in the land of Oz. The creator of *The Wonderful Wizard of Oz* was L. Frank Baum, an American writer, actor and auteur. The first Oz book, which he produced alongside illustrator W.W. Denslow, appeared in 1900. It topped the children's bestseller lists for two years, and the partnership would produce another thirteen novels set in the imaginary land. Years later, Baum's sons revealed how Oz had got its name. As their father sat in his study, racking his brain for something suitable, his eyes alighted on a filing cabinet. Had he fixed on the top drawer, we might be talking about the Wizard of AN. As it was, he looked at the bottom draw which contained files O to Z.

Here's looking at you, George

For many film fans, there has never been a bigger star than Humphrey Bogart. Indeed, at the end of the last century the

American Film Institute named him the greatest screen actor of all time. The world-weary and hard-boiled persona combined with a brooding sexual tension (particularly opposite Lauren Bacall, to whom he was married for the last twelve years of his life) to ensure that his performances remain as enthralling today as on their day of release. Yet at least two – and reputedly three – of his greatest roles were due to have gone to George Raft, a cinematic rival whose fame has lasted less well.

Born in New York in 1899, Bogie had been expected to follow a medical career until he was thrown out of school. Instead, he went into the Navy Reserve, where the story goes that he got his trade-mark lisp when a shackled prisoner struck him in the mouth during an escape attempt. Others, though, claim that this was a story put about in later years by his film studio and that he actually got a large wooden splinter in his lip when he was twelve years old.

After leaving the navy, Bogart started managing a theatre company and helped out at a New York film studio owned by a family friend. His early stage appearances weren't promising – one critic, Alexander Woollcott, described him as 'inadequate' – but by 1930 Bogie had secured a contract with Fox. However, he was released within two years and he would have to wait until 1936 for his first bona fide hit, playing Duke Mantee in *The Petrified Forest*. Warner Bros, the producers, used him widely throughout the rest of the decade, usually as a smart-talking gangster.

In 1939 he appeared in *Invisible Stripes* alongside George

Raft, who was one of cinema's biggest stars of the 1930s, playing in a series of gangster films. His authenticity may have had something to do with the friendship he had built up with 'Bugsy' Siegel during the childhood they shared on the streets of New York. Raft and Bogart would double up again for *They Drive by Night* in 1940.

However, Raft's golden touch then seems to have deserted him, and it was Bogart who was the chief beneficiary. Raft was offered the role of Roy Earle in 1941's *High Sierra* but didn't like the character's fate so turned it down. Bogie stepped in, the film was a massive critical and box office success, and Bogart, now in his 40s, was accepted into Hollywood's senior ranks. The following year, Raft was wanted to play Sam Spade in *The Maltese Falcon*, a remake of a 1931 film. Raft had doubts about the director so passed on the part, and again Bogart took over. It has become widely accepted as one of the greatest films of all time. Raft reputedly completed his hat-trick of own goals by rejecting the role of Rick Blaine in *Casablanca* in 1942, though there's some dispute over whether this part of the tale is apocryphal. Whatever the truth, *Casablanca* is one of cinema's best loved and most quoted (and indeed, misquoted) films, regularly appearing in the ten greatest films of all time. Bogie also received an Oscar nomination for it.

As Raft's star declined, Bogie's remained in the ascendant, his career taking in such classics as *The Big Sleep* (1946), *Key Largo* (1948), *The African Queen* (for which he got an Oscar in 1951) and *The Caine Mutiny* (1954). As for

Raft, he became the subject of Stone Wallace's 2008 book: *George Raft – The Man Who Would Be Bogart*.

Luck among the haystacks

Peter O'Toole is one of the great British actors of his generation, more than holding his own (on stage and screen, to say nothing of at the bar) alongside contemporaries as prestigious as Laurence Olivier, Richard Harris and Richard Burton. In 1962 he took the lead in David Lean's *Lawrence of Arabia*, achieving global superstardom with a performance rated as the greatest of all time by *Premiere* magazine in 2006. He was seven times Oscar-nominated before finally picking up an honorary Academy Award in 2003. Yet his beginnings were relatively humble, growing up in Leeds as the son of a bookmaker. His first giant step towards acceptance as an actor came courtesy of the unlikely fallout of a night on the town.

In 1952 O'Toole paid a visit to Stratford-upon-Avon with his old chum, Patrick Oliver. There they took in the Royal Shakespeare Company's production of *King Lear* before embarking on a session of boozing. Having no rooms to go to, the two decided to sleep among some hay bales they had spotted in a nearby field. Their initial delight at the unexpected warmth of the bedding dissipated a little when they realised the hay was actually the padding to great stinking blocks of fertiliser.

When they awoke the following morning, dishevelled and

no doubt rather malodorous, they hitched a lift on a truck bound for London, where they were staying at a hostel on Tottenham Court Road. Dropped off at Euston Station, they were only a short way along the walk to their digs when O'Toole was rather taken with the elaborate portico of one particular building that turned out to be the Royal Academy of Dramatic Art, the nation's premier training ground for actors.

Despite his unkempt appearance, O'Toole went into the building while Oliver remained outside. Once inside, O'Toole was captivated by a bronze bust of one of his heroes, George Bernard Shaw. He entertained the security guard with some anecdotes about the venerable old playwright, then noticed that another elderly gentleman had appeared on the scene, seeking out the source of all the laughter.

O'Toole engaged in animated conversation with this man, who turned out to be RADA's Principal, Sir Kenneth Barnes. Barnes was obviously struck by the young man's remarkable charisma and when O'Toole voiced his hopes of one day studying at the institution, Barnes fast-tracked him through the elaborate application process that normally lasted months, instead offering him an interview that very day. An audition was then hastily arranged for the end of the week, where O'Toole was expected to perform one audition piece from a list of set texts and another of his own choice. He was delighted to see that among the set texts was a scene from Shaw's *Pygmalion*, an old O'Toole family favourite that he knew back to front. Being in the right place at just the right moment combined with his undoubted talent to ensure that he was one of the less than 3 per cent of successful applicants to the Academy, and in double quick time to boot.

Wooden acting

Harrison Ford was a jobbing actor struggling to support his family when he decided that he should find himself a more reliable trade. He trained as a carpenter and began working for a number of Hollywood celebrities. Among them was George Lucas, the director of *Star Wars*, whose influence was to make Ford one of the biggest stars in the world.

Ford was born in 1942 and had a comfortable upbringing in Illinois. He studied acting at Wisconsin's Ripon College, where he became heavily involved with local theatre groups. In 1964, married and with two young children, he headed for California to make it to the Big Time. But rather than instant stardom, he found himself living on minor roles in minor films and a smattering of television work. He desperately needed another source of income, and decided that he would be best served by carpentry.

It was a job for which he had some considerable talent, and he found the woodworking commissions were flowing far better than the acting ones. One particular client was so impressed that he recommended Ford to his friend Sérgio Mendes, the famed Brazilian musician. So began a new phase of Ford's career that saw him working for a number of big names. Among them was the emerging film director,

George Lucas, who reputedly wanted some new cabinets. The two men got talking about Ford's acting aspirations and Ford ended up with a supporting role in Lucas's 1973 film, *American Graffiti*.

Even better was to follow, though. Two years later, Lucas called on Ford to read lines for other actors at castings for *Star Wars*. Spielberg, a friend of Lucas, persuaded the director to give Ford a chance in the pivotal role of Han Solo, the smooth-talking space smuggler. The movie was released in 1977 and became the highest grossing film of all time, attracting an army of fans whose devotion seemed to know no end.

As *Star Wars* established itself as a phenomenon and then an institution, Ford's own career went into orbit too. He starred in the equally successful follow-ups, *The Empire Strikes Back* and *Return of the Jedi*. Spielberg then cast him as the lead in the hugely popular *Indiana Jones* series (which was intended to have been taken by Tom Selleck) and a long list of other hits includes *Air Force One*, *Blade Runner*, *Clear and Present Danger*, *Patriot Games*, *Presumed Innocent*, *The Fugitive*, *What Lies Beneath* and *Witness*. His movies have grossed over $6 billion worldwide. Though should it all end tomorrow, he must be comforted to know he has a trade to fall back on.

An offer he couldn't refuse

The book of *The Godfather*, the gritty story of an Italian-American organised crime dynasty, sold in its millions and the series of films that derived from it are regarded as some of the finest to have come out of Hollywood. The book's author, Mario Puzo, was a respected but commercially unsuccessful author whose moment seemed to have come and gone before a chance meeting in the offices of a magazine for which he wrote.

Puzo was born in 1920 into an immigrant family in the notorious Hell's Kitchen area of New York. He had a tough upbringing but fell in love with literature. In 1950 his first short story was published. Five years later, a novel, *The Dark Arena*, appeared, followed ten years later by *The Fortunate Pilgrim*. Both were critical successes but failed to set the cash tills alight.

Puzo, married and with five children to support, spent twenty years working for the government. But in 1963 he went freelance as a writer and journalist, working for an array of titles including a number of pulp magazines. Here he picked up countless stories of the has-to-be-seen-to-be-believed activities of real-life gangsters, though he always claimed he had never met a mobster himself before he wrote his book. In 1965 he was in the offices of one of the more respectable magazines he wrote for, and was regaling a small crowd of its employees with his second-hand tales of nefarious doings. It so happened that an editor from Putnam, the famous New York publishers, was passing through and overheard Puzo. He was knocked out by the tales and offered Puzo a $5,000 advance to go away and write a book on the subject. *The Godfather* was the result.

Published in 1969, *The Godfather* topped the bestseller charts for 67 weeks, selling 21 million copies. It was later made into two hugely successful films by Francis Ford Coppola, with Puzo picking up Oscars for each of the screenplays. Puzo always considered he'd written the book 'below his talents' and had regarded it as very much a commercial proposition. Instead he established one of the greatest literary and cinematic legacies of American culture.

Not just a pretty face

Mel Gibson has had some well-documented problems with alcohol abuse, but, in part, his big break came about because of a big night out. Gibson was born in New York but his family moved to Australia when he was twelve years old. He went on to study at the National Institute of Dramatic Art in Sydney and started to win good notices for his performances on stage, television and in independent film. Having got himself an agent, in 1979 he was put up for a part in a low-rent, post-apocalyptic thriller called *Mad Max*. It would change his life.

A boozy night on the tiles was never going to be the ideal preparation for an audition. But, perhaps feeling the need for a little Dutch courage, that was how Gibson chose to ready himself. When an altercation in a bar room turned into an all-out brawl, it must have seemed like an even more foolish undertaking. Gibson took a beating and awoke the next morning to see an unfamiliar face staring back from the mirror, one that was swollen and dreadfully bruised. In his own words, he resembled 'a black and blue pumpkin'. Feeling naturally downhearted at this turn of events, he could find little enthusiasm for his audition, but because he had a friend who was also going to try out, he made the decision to go.

The casting agent was seemingly taken with the rough-and-tumble look that Gibson had been forced to adopt. He was sent home with instructions to return in two weeks' time, his ears ringing with these encouraging words: 'We need freaks.' He duly came back a fortnight later, his injuries having healed and looking much more like the handsome film star with whom we are familiar. Nonetheless, his 'pumpkin' styling had clearly made an impression, for he won the lead role of George Miller.

The part proved to be Gibson's big break. The film cost a few hundred thousand dollars to make but made back over a hundred million. Two sequels followed, establishing Gibson as box office gold and ensuring his future in Hollywood. His subsequent career has encompassed directing as well as acting and has been characterised by unpredictability, his work ranging from the hugely successful *Lethal Weapon* series to the Oscar-winning *Braveheart* and the controversial *The Passion of the Christ*.

Croft's original

Dad's Army tells the story of the loveably haphazard Home

Guard in the imaginary town of Walmington-on-Sea during the Second World War. It's one of the landmark comedies of British TV, a beautifully observed take on the nation's darkest days that reflects the much-spoken-of British ability to keep a sense of humour in a crisis. The programme is justly recognised as a great example of ensemble acting, but at its core is the inverted relationship between Captain Mainwaring, the pompous Little Englander extraordinaire, and his second-in-command, the debonair, ex-public school Sergeant Wilson. It was a relationship of pure comedy gold and so, inevitably, owed its existence more to luck than any judgement by senior BBC executives.

Jimmy Perry had written a pilot episode in 1967 and came up with a shortlist of actors he envisioned for the major roles. In his mind, he saw Arthur Lowe in the role of Sergeant Wilson (the part that John Le Mesurier so memorably made his own), with Robert Dorning playing Captain Mainwaring. Lowe and Dorning had already established a strong partnership in the comedies *Pardon the Expression* and *Turn Out the Lights*.

However, the powers-that-be weren't keen on Lowe being involved at all, apparently because of his close ties with ITV. This was a period when the BBC still exhibited a somewhat superior attitude towards its commercial rival. So it was that they offered the role of Mainwaring first to Thorley Walters, who was probably best known for his appearances in several Hammer horrors and in classic British comedy films like *Blue Murder at St Trinian's*. When he rejected it, the BBC turned to Jon Pertwee, who also turned it down as he had existing commitments both in the UK and US. It would turn out to be a fortuitous decision for Pertwee too (whose cousin, Bill, featured in *Dad's Army* as Hodges, the Air Raid Warden), for it allowed him to take up the opportunity of replacing Patrick Troughton as Dr Who. With the short-list for the role thus decimated, it was only then that Perry persuaded the producer, Michael Mills, and his co-writer, David Croft, to take another look at Lowe. They caved in and gave Lowe the job. Meanwhile a senior BBC executive, Huw Wheldon, told the press that his assumption was that Lowe would play Wilson and Le Mesurier would play Mainwaring. Thankfully, he wasn't responsible for final casting.

The show's success was immediate, with viewing figures peaking at 18.5 million viewers per episode (including the Queen Mother, whose favourite programme it was). Eighty episodes were shown over nine series and there were also spin-off films and stage shows. When asked to explain the show's success, Perry responded: 'The secret was that everything was right. It was one of those rare things: the cast was right, the time was right, the subject was right.'

Break a leg!

Shirley MacLaine is something of a Hollywood icon, a fine actress, singer and hoofer who has also carved out a career as a writer. It's difficult to believe that she wouldn't have made it to the big time by dint of energy alone, but her big break actually came as the result of another star's big break.

MacLaine was born Shirley MacLean Beaty in 1934 in Richmond, Virginia, but changed her name when she moved to New York after graduating from high school. As a child she was a talented ballerina, but as she got into her teens she realised that a career as a professional was probably a step beyond her. Ironically, she also suffered a terrible injury to her ankle.

In 1954 *The Pajama Game* was about to open on Broadway, starring Carol Haney who was a cohort of both Gene Kelly and Bob Fosse. When Fosse took on the choreography for *The Pajama Game*, he suggested Haney be given a role, and the director, George Abbott, was so impressed by her that she was cast in the lead as Gladys Hotchkiss. Haney won great acclaim for her performance and a Tony Award too.

MacLaine was her understudy and was well aware of Haney's reputation for physical durability; word had it that Haney never missed a performance. As the run went on, MacLaine grew increasingly frustrated at the lack of opportunity and was about to hand in her resignation to try her luck in a rival production, *Can Can*. Then the unthinkable happened and Haney fractured her ankle. MacLaine took over the role and, despite an initially frosty reception from audiences desperate to see Haney, soon won the crowds over with her high-octane performances.

A little while into her run, Hal B. Wallis, the legendary

producer, came to see the show. Boasting a spectacular CV that included *Casablanca*, Wallis saw star quality in the young MacLaine and immediately booked her for a screen-test that resulted in a long-term contract with Paramount. Within three months she was filming on the set of *The Trouble with Harry* (for which she received a Golden Globe) and in 1958 received her first Oscar nomination for *Some Came Running*. A second nomination came in 1960 for the much admired *The Apartment*, and there was another three years later for *Irma la Douce*. In 1975 the Academy nominated her in the documentary category for *The Other Half of the Sky: A China Memoir* and in 1983 she finally picked up the Best Actress award for *Terms of Endearment*. She has subsequently appeared in a host of other well-loved films including *Steel Magnolias*, *Postcards from the Edge* and *In Her Shoes*. It was a stellar rise that began with a role she never really expected to play. But, as they say, them's the breaks.

First impressions last

Grauman's Chinese Theatre at 6925 Hollywood Boulevard is one of Hollywood's great institutions. For many years the venue of the Oscars ceremony, it's perhaps most famous for its concrete blocks bearing the hand- and foot-prints of many of cinema's biggest names. The tradition began when a sex siren of the silent screen took an unplanned walk in the unset cement of the theatre's forecourt.

Sid Grauman was the man behind the theatre. He decided to build it in 1926 following the success of his nearby Egyptian Theatre and persuaded Douglas Fairbanks, Mary Pickford and Howard Schenck to co-fund the project. Designed by the architectural firm of Meyer and Holler to suggest a Chinese pagoda, it took eighteen months to construct and opened in May 1927.

Shortly afterwards Norma Talmadge visited the theatre. Though largely forgotten now, Talmadge was a superstar at the time, with silent classics to her name like *Smilin' Through*, *Secrets* and *The Lady*. Unaware that a slab of concrete at the front of the building was still wet, she walked straight across it. Grauman was quick to see the publicity potential of the accidental footprint, and roped in Fairbanks and Pickford to add their stardust-sprinkled prints too.

The forecourt soon became a landmark for visitors, and Grauman invited a host of other famous names to contribute to it. Jean Klossner, who was responsible for the original cement lay, was employed to oversee footprint ceremonies for the next 35 years. Today there are imprints from almost 200 Hollywood celebrities. While most use their feet and hands or inscribe an autograph, others are more imaginative. Harold Lloyd left an imprint of his glasses, Groucho Marx a cigar, Jimmy Durante his nose, Champion the Wonder Horse his hooves, and Daniel Radcliffe a magic wand.

For Norma Talmadge the emergence of the talkies was cruel, and she was among its biggest casualties as she failed to repeat her successes of the silent era. Yet while her films may now be rarely seen, her legacy at Grauman's Chinese Theatre is permanently preserved in concrete.

CHAPTER 6

Criminal Negligence

Thankfully, the Moriarty-esque criminal mastermind is a rare thing and he's far outnumbered by your run-of-the-mill n'er-do-well blessed with considerably fewer gifts in the brains department. Nonetheless, instances of truly spectacular ineptitude are relatively uncommon and should be cherished, especially by those working on the side of law and order. Policing is an unforgiving job but, just occasionally, a criminal will endeavour to brighten up a policeman's lot. Julius Comroe Jr, the esteemed American medic and teacher, described serendipity as 'looking in a haystack for a needle and discovering a farmer's daughter'. In the case of this chapter, simply substitute the farmer's daughter for a miscreant.

A bum rap

In September 2008, a 26-year-old woman was put on trial in Germany for armed robbery. Alas for the defendant, her rather rotund derriere proved to be her undoing, as she proved that it's easier said than done to put your crimes behind you.

The intrepid raider carried out her attack on a bank in Norf, a town in western Germany, getting away with around €15,000. From the witness statements police took at the time, one thing became clear – the culprit had a 'very large' backside.

Several weeks later the same woman returned to the same bank for what she must have thought would be another easy payday. But as luck would have it, she was followed into the queue by a 61-year-old man who had been present for her first robbery. In a moment of flashback, he recognised her distinctive buttocks, later commenting that he'd 'never forget something that big'. He called the police and they arrived on the scene to arrest the suspect, who was searched and found to be in possession of a ski mask and handgun. Charged with firearms offences and attempted robbery, she faced ten years in jail.

Her case may at least provide one lesson for the criminal class. If you get away with it once, it doesn't pay to be too cheeky.

That's curtains for them

It was on 29 November 1978 that David Goodhall and two lady friends spent the afternoon drinking in South Yorkshire ahead of a shoplifting spree of admirable ineptitude. For their own self-respect, it's to be hoped they were able to blame the alcohol, because their plan was found to be severely lacking in the ... well, planning department.

Buoyed by Dutch courage, the daring trio travelled into the Barnsley branch of British Home Stores, the venerable old department store. Deciding to bypass small, easily concealable items, they crammed a pair of curtains into a carrier bag before splitting up and each leaving by a different exit. It was a classic divide-and-conquer tactic – there was simply no way, even if their theft was spotted, that the in-store security would be able to cope with such a cunning strategy.

At least that's what they might have assumed, had it not been for the fact that the store was hosting a convention of store detectives that day. Each of the trio was picked up the moment they tried to leave the store, with Goodhall, the ringleader, finding himself surrounded by eight fully-trained security experts.

In a similar vein, in 2009 a robber reportedly held up a man at gunpoint in the toilets of a conference centre in Pennsylvania. The victim handed over his wallet and telephone before he was able to alert his colleagues and give chase. To add insult to injury, the victim was forced to drop his trousers. However, had the assailant been a little more observant, he would have noticed a gun holstered to the victim's leg. The victim was one John Comparetto, a retired police chief, who was attending a convention of narcotics police along with 300 other officers. His attacker was soon under arrest. Nonetheless, the ill-prepared criminal was keen to maintain an aura of invincibility, allegedly telling a waiting journalist outside his trial: 'I'm smooth.'

Another thief who should have staked out his scene of crime more thoroughly was one Colin Baggs, who attempted to break into a car parked outside his garage in Frome, Somerset, in 1987. Alas, he failed to spot the two police officers sitting inside the vehicle.

Sausage-fingers

In August 1986, three police officers led by Daniel Sweetwood were on the night shift in Kansas City, Missouri. In the early hours they received word from a 911 operator of an emergency. Unfortunately, the caller hadn't been able to describe what was wrong before the line had gone dead, but the operator was able to employ a computer system to identify the address from where the call had come.

Not knowing what they were going to find once they reached their destination, the officers approached with some trepidation. To their amazement, they found that the property housed a stash of dirty money, drugs and weapons. To top it off, two women suspected of drug couriering were present at the scene and immediately arrested.

Unable to explain who had given them such a ripe tip-off, it soon emerged that it was a member of the drug ring itself who had made the emergency 911 call. The reason? They had actually been trying to contact their 'Mr Big', whose number began 921, and managed to mis-dial.

A prison of their own making

On the evening of 27 September 1989 a crack team of three young thieves set out to break into an unoccupied pick-up truck in the town of Larkspur, California. However, the gang, led by eighteen-year-old Stephen Le, was spotted by the occupants of a nearby house, who notified the police.

Soon a police car was on the scene, but the men, judging youth to be on their side, chose to scarper for all they were worth. They were sprinting along the road but their pursuers were making ground, so they were left with a difficult decision when they saw, running parallel to the road, a chain-link fence crowned with some particularly unappealing barbed wire. The would-be car bandits decided to chance their arm and hurl themselves over it.

Alas for them, the fence marked the outer boundary of San Quentin Prison, the infamous Californian correctional centre. Sensibly realising that the game was up, they waited for the police, who arrested them for auto burglary and trespassing on state property. As one police officer insightfully observed: 'People just don't break in to prison every day.'

Customer service

We all like to feel like that our banks are looking out for us, but most of us accept that there are limits. Not so for one decidedly optimistic robber operating in Pittsfield, Massachusetts in the 1970s.

It was early December 1974 when a 33-year-old man decided to go for an unscheduled meeting at a branch of the City Savings Bank on the town's West Housatonic Street shortly before opening time. He cornered one of the tellers and made a demand for cash. She astutely noticed that two of her colleagues were about to enter the bank, and asked the robber if she might go and tell these 'customers' that the bank wasn't yet open.

He condescended to agree, so off she popped to the front door, mouthing a code word known to all the bank's employees as a sign that a crime was in progress. The teller's two colleagues promptly left the bank to find a phone and call the police.

Meanwhile, the master criminal, now in possession of close to $10,000, realised that he had overlooked how he might make a timely escape from the crime scene. Having granted the teller a favour, he decided to ask one of her in return. Could she possibly loan him her car? The teller agreed and the robber made a hasty exit. Within a few minutes, the police were on the scene and she was able to furnish them with a complete description of the vehicle transporting the miscreant. He was caught within minutes.

Cheque mate

It's right that crime shouldn't pay, but every now and then a criminal experiences such a dose of bad luck that you can't help but feel a slight pang of sympathy.

Take one Frances Nigro, who in September 1987 stole a cheque written out to one Linda Brandimato as well as a wallet containing Brandimato's identification. Nigro promptly set out to dishonestly cash the cheque and made for a drive-through bank in Monroe Township, New Jersey. Up she went to the first available teller, handing over the cheque and all the appropriate paperwork. As luck would have it, the teller she had chosen was Linda Brandimato. Nigro attempted to make off in her car but Brandimato called the police, who soon had the culprit in custody.

On a similar theme, Diana Klos, a shop worker in Irvington, New Jersey, was somewhat taken aback to find herself serving a customer making a purchase with a stolen credit card. The rightful owner of the card: Diana Klos. Klos called up her boss on the shop's internal phone system and the two chased the thief out of the store and on to the street, where two policemen were ideally situated to make an arrest.

A twist in the tale

In the summer of 1980 a convict called Tonino Lacordia made a daring escape by scaling the wall of the Madonna Del Freddo prison, situated near Chietti in the Abruzzo region of Italy. As he made his leap for freedom, Lacordia fell awkwardly and badly twisted his ankle. Unable to go on the run, he went on the hobble instead, covering a distance of a few miles over several painful hours. At least he was able to console himself that he was in a reasonably rural area where detection would be unlikely.

As the pain from his injured foot got worse, he realised he had no option but to stop for a rest. He found what seemed to be a suitably remote cottage and knocked on the door. One can only imagine his surprise when the door was opened by a strangely familiar face. It was the policeman who had made Lacordia's original arrest and who had subsequently decided to rent a property in the countryside to forget about the criminal side of life for a week or two.

Metal detecting

4 November 1933 is truly a red letter day in the annals of criminal ineptitude. The crime in question was carried out in Paris, long regarded as the city of high fashion. On this occasion our hero's taste in dress was seriously flawed.

The unnamed burglar set out on that particular evening to rob the house of a renowned antiques dealer. Many lesser criminal minds might have concluded that silence and stealth would be the order of the day, but not this thief. He seems to have decided that, lest he come face to face with his victim, he stood the best chance if he had the wherewithal to terrify him. To this end he decided to dispense with a more traditional outfit, such as a striped jersey, face mask and accessorised swag bag, in favour of a 15th-century suit of armour.

It was, some might suggest, almost inevitable that a man

in medieval armour might attract unwanted attention while attempting to drift unnoticed around a Paris town house. And so it proved. As he ascended the stairs, the thief's clanking alerted the house-owner to some mischief. A confrontation ensued, in which the criminal was at a disadvantage because of his inability to manoeuvre easily. The antique dealer seized the opportunity to drop a vintage sideboard on the intruder.

The thief crashed to the ground and, his metal suit now dented, was even less capable of rapid movement. Sensing the game was up, he awaited the police who promptly arrested him. He was eventually freed from his armour the following day.

Love is blind

'If at first you don't succeed, try, try again,' wrote Thomas H. Palmer in the 1840s. Admirable sentiment though it is, there's a time to know when to give up, something that Terrence Bell of Portsmouth came to realise in 1980 when seven attempts to kill his wife went entirely unnoticed.

With an insurance policy worth a quarter of a million pounds at stake, his first two tries involved mercury poisoning. The first dose rolled out of a fruit flan that he had prepared for the good woman. On the second occasion, she consumed a laced mackerel with no obvious ill effect. After a decent hiatus, his plans to push her off a cliff in Yugoslavia failed when she flatly refused to go near the edge. A re-run several weeks later at Beachy Head ended in similar frustration. Next came a couple of arson attempts. On the first occasion, a kindly neighbour realised there was a blaze and broke into the Bell house to extinguish the flames. The next attempt caused extensive damage to the property but none at all to Mrs Bell. The final murder attempt lacked subtlety. Mr Bell explained that his car had brake problems and suggested that his wife might stand in the road while he drove towards her to test them. She obligingly did so, but leapt to safety at the vital moment.

Mr Bell admitted defeat and handed himself in to the custody of Hampshire police. His wife was amazed at the subsequent revelations, having failed to spot anything wrong in her relationship.

CHAPTER 7

The Medicine Cabinet

The notion of serendipity has been the focal point of a debate among scientists for many years. For some, the very idea seems to undermine the role played by dedicated researchers who make discoveries by informed trial and error and intensive observation. Others, though, accept that sometimes a scientist is looking for one thing and simply stumbles upon something quite different. It's then that the scientist's sagacity becomes important – the ability to recognise the potential of their discovery and to develop it into something truly useful. No lesser light than Louis Pasteur once observed: 'In the field of observations, chance favours only the prepared mind.'

Barking up the right tree

Malaria remains one of the world's most deadly threats, an infectious disease that kills up to three million people a year, principally in tropical and sub-tropical regions. Spread by mosquito bites, there remains no effective vaccination against it, but we do at least have some effective treatments.

The first of these was quinine, the therapeutic effects of which were discovered by luck in the 17th century. It remained the anti-malarial treatment of choice until well into the 20th century.

Quinine is derived from the bark of the cinchona tree, a species found in high-altitude areas from Colombia down to Bolivia. Some time in the early 1600s, one of Peru's native Quechua Indians contracted malaria amid the high Andean jungle. Suffering from a symptomatic fever, he needed to take on water. He found a pool of bitter-tasting water overhung by cinchona trees and in desperation drank from it, despite the Quechua believing the cinchona to be poisonous. Miraculously his malarial symptoms receded. He took back word of his recovery, and his tribe developed the bark of the cinchona as a remedy.

At this period Peru was full of Roman Catholic missionaries venturing from Europe to the New World. They knew of malaria themselves, for the disease was endemic around Rome, among other European areas, and had even claimed the lives of several popes. Around 1630 a Jesuit apothecary, Agostino Salumbrino, was based in Lima, Peru's capital. He saw how the Quechua used the cinchona bark to combat the disease and sent a sample back to Italy. Within a few years there was a thriving trade in cinchona between the two continents, with the bark ground up and dissolved in a sweet drink or wine. Quinine was the first chemical compound to be successfully used to combat an infectious disease.

Enough to put you to sleep

Surgery is never a joyous prospect but it must have been terrifying before the advent of effective anaesthetics. The idea of 'knocking out' a patient before invasive surgery has been around since at least the days of ancient Egypt, when boys about to be circumcised were half-strangled to render them unconscious. But it wasn't until the 19th century that real progress was made and modern anaesthetics as we understand them came into general use. Serendipity had a large role to play in the development of two common anaesthetics: nitrous oxide and ether.

Nitrous oxide (or laughing gas) was discovered around 1799 by Humphry Davy, a young English scientist investigating how gases might be used in medicine. Inhaling sixteen quarts of the gas, he, not surprisingly, lapsed into hysterical guffawing before being rendered 'absolutely intoxicated'. Human nature being what it is, the medical world was sceptical about the practical applications of the gas, but the entertainment world realised it might make a hell of a good show. So it was that travelling shows would invite members of the public to inhale the nitrous oxide to everyone's great amusement.

At one such show at Hartford, Connecticut in 1844, the *inhalee* was one Samuel Cooley. However, his *joie de vivre* lasted only momentarily; he soon became aggressive, and a scuffle broke out. Eventually he calmed and resumed his seat in the audience next to his friend, Horace Wells, a dentist. A little while later, Wells noticed a great outpouring of blood from a deep cut in Cooley's leg. Cooley, though, was oblivious, at least until the effects of the gas had worn off.

Wells grasped the implications and began experimenting with the gas, having one of his own molars painlessly removed while under the influence. Wells might have become a very rich and famous man were it not for his over-eagerness at a public demonstration in Boston, when he attempted to extract a patient's tooth before the gas had taken hold. Joe Public heard the screams and was unconvinced that they represented a bright new future.

A few years later a student of Wells, William Morton, successfully demonstrated the benefits of ether (and specifically diethyl ether) as an anaesthetic by removing a tumour from a patient's neck at the very same hospital in Boston. However, a lifelong controversy was to follow as Morton's partner, Charles Jackson, claimed it was he who had originated the use of ether. In a scene reminiscent of a Victorian gothic horror novel, he described how he had been working in his lab in the winter of 1841 when one of his experiments smashed and he was overcome by noxious chlorine fumes. In an attempt to counteract the chlorine, he took alternate lung-fulls of ether and ammonia, which he found to be pleasingly soothing. The following day he inhaled still more ether in the hope of easing his painful throat. By chance he had stumbled on a gas that not only desensitised the subject to pain but could even produce unconsciousness. James Simpson reputedly discovered the anaesthetising properties of chloroform in a similar fashion in 1847 when he and a roomful of his students inhaled the vapours after one of the class clumsily knocked over a bottle of the substance.

Listen to your heart

It's often said that necessity is the mother of invention. In the early 19th century a French doctor, René Théophile Hyacinthe Laënnec, was confronted with a patient whose heart he needed to listen to. Physical constraints and social mores made traditional methods impossible, so the doctor contrived a new approach using some papers he had to hand. The result, after a period of refinement, was the stethoscope, an instrument that revolutionised the medical profession.

Laënnec was born in Brittany in 1781 and studied medicine in Nantes under the guidance of his uncle, Gauillaime-François Laënnec, before continuing his studies in Paris. In 1816 he was working at the Hôpital Necker, where among his patients was a young woman displaying symptoms of heart disease. One method of diagnosis, known as percussion, involved tapping the chest with the fingers and listening to the sounds produced in order to identify any abnormality. However, the patient was somewhat obese, rendering this method ineffective. An alternative was for the doctor to put his ear to her breast and listen to her heartbeat directly, but the social conventions of the period made this extremely awkward, particularly when patient and doctor were both young.

At that moment he remembered an old acoustic

experiment he was once shown – how if you scratched the end of a length of wood with a pin, it could be distinctly heard by applying one's ear to the other end. With that in mind, he rolled up the papers he was carrying into a cylinder, applied one end to the region of the woman's heart and put his ear against the other. He could hear her heartbeat with striking clarity. Indeed, the sound was clearer than he had experienced with any other method he had employed.

Laënnec ran with his idea, building his first prototype stethoscope out of wood. The hollow cylinder was around 25cm long and 2.5cm wide. In time he modified it so that it consisted of three detachable segments. Using this new instrument in long-term studies of patients allowed him to associate particular sound patterns with specific heart and lung conditions. Many of his classifications remain in use today.

He went public with his invention in 1895, though it was many years before the medical profession in general took it to their, or indeed their patients', hearts. Laënnec was nonetheless convinced of its importance. On his death (in 1826 from cavitating tuberculosis – a diagnosis confirmed by his own invention), he bequeathed his personal stethoscope to his nephew, describing it as 'the greatest legacy of my life'.

Milking the opportunity

Smallpox was an awful way to die, an infectious virus that preyed on humans, leaving the victim wracked with fever and their body covered with pus-filled blisters. No cure was ever discovered and it carried a fatality rate of some 30 per cent. Survivors were often left with unsightly scars and a high risk of blindness. The disease was rife in Europe until the 18th century, when it claimed around 400,000 lives a year, and it's estimated to have killed in excess of 300 million people worldwide in the 20th century. It was a class-blind assailant too, taking anyone from peasants to monarchs. However, in the late 18th century, Edward Jenner, an English doctor, was pointed towards one group of people who seemed to escape its clutches. This discovery led to the formulation of an effective inoculation against the disease.

Edward Jenner was born in Gloucestershire in 1749 and himself survived a childhood attack of smallpox. As he got older, he set his heart on a career in medicine and embarked on an apprenticeship in London with John Hunter, a prominent surgeon. When Jenner returned to Gloucestershire to set up surgery, he recalled an observation that a local milkmaid had made to him in his younger days. She had told him that she was safe from smallpox because she had suffered cowpox. From the mid-1770s he made a detailed study and realised that it was true – hardly any milkmaids were afflicted, even if they were in close contact with sufferers.

This chance discovery led him to believe that the cowpox virus must offer some immunity against the much more serious smallpox. His subsequent studies revealed that it was one particular strain of cowpox that offered protection, and then for a fairly short period in its life-cycle. Yet the medical authorities of the time were sceptical as to the relevance of his work. Or at least they were until 1796, when he somehow persuaded a family to allow him to inject their eight-year-old child, James Phipps, with cowpox matter from an infected milkmaid, Sarah Nelmes, and then, several months later, with the smallpox virus. As Jenner had hoped, Phipps didn't develop the latter disease. Cowpox in Gloucestershire rather inconveniently waned over the next two years, so it wasn't until 1798 that Jenner could further verify his thesis. It's interesting to note that he coined the word *vaccine* in 1803, deriving it from the Latin name for cowpox, *variolae vaccinae* (*vacca* being the word for cow). The philanthropic Jenner never sought a patent for his vaccine, believing that the general good was best served by allowing it to be freely available.

Europe was soon rid of the spectre of smallpox but it continued to do enormous damage in the developing world through most of the last century. However, in 1980 the World Health Organization confirmed that by a process of vaccination, the disease had been eradicated from the world, the first time that man has been able to 'remove' a disease in such a way.

Throwing light on a problem

From the late 1850s, much work was undertaken by physicists into the effects of passing electrical currents through different gases in vacuum tubes, and in particular the occurrence of phosphorescent light. Research in this area would ultimately result in the invention, among other things, of neon signage and the cathode ray tube used in televisions. More surprisingly, when a German physicist attempted to replicate the experiments of other scientists in the field, he discovered X-rays.

Wilhelm Röntgen was a German-born academic. In the early 1890s Heinrich Hertz and Philipp Lenard had invented gas-filled tubes with, respectively, thin metallic foils and aluminium windows, through which cathode rays (streams of electrons emitted from a cathode) could pass to produce a beam of light on a suitable screen a few centimetres away. In November 1895 Röntgen was carrying out his own studies on cathode ray tubes, during which he constructed a black cardboard cover to block out all light from the tubes.

Satisfied that this black-out case was doing the trick, he was about to move his detecting screen (which was coated in barium platinocyanide) into range before beginning his experiments. To his amazement, though, he saw that a faint green light was already evident upon the screen, despite it being at least three feet from the tube. He double-checked the black cardboard casing and found it was securely in place. Realising that the green light could thus not be a product of cathode rays, he spent the next few weeks trying to get to the bottom of this mysterious new radiation. He discovered that the rays could pass through books, blocks of wood and even thick aluminium plates. Furthermore, he found that if he held his hand in the path of the rays, a skeletal image was produced on the screen. He published his paper, 'On a New Kind of Rays', in December 1895 and, still unable to identify the type of radiation, referred to it as X-rays, a name that stuck. Before the end of the year, an image of the hand of his wife, Anne Bertha, was captured on a photographic plate to become the first published X-ray of a human body part.

The medical world was quick to adopt the new technology and X-rays became a staple tool of diagnosis in hospitals throughout the world. Röntgen won the first Nobel Prize for Physics in 1901.

From sweet potato to sweet lovin'

There have been few medical discoveries that have had a deeper social impact than that of the oral contraceptive pill. Indeed, its significance to the revolution in sexual mores that swept through the Western world in the second half of the 20th century was reflected by its being known simply as the Pill. It was discovered by Dr Carl Djerassi, an organic chemist who admitted that 'an oral contraceptive was not in anyone's thoughts' when he created it.

Carl Djerassi was born in Vienna in 1923 but came to the USA with his mother when he was sixteen. Having completed a PhD at the University of Wisconsin-Madison, he obtained US citizenship in 1945. In 1949 he was working for a company called Syntex in Mexico City, under one George Rosenkranz. Syntex had been established several years earlier expressly to manufacture progesterone, a key hormone in the female menstrual cycle. One of the Syntex founders, Russell Marker, had found a way to synthetically produce progesterone from sapogenins, a type of steroid present in certain breeds of Mexican yams (naturally).

Marker, though, had left Syntex by the time Djerassi joined. Djerassi was appointed to lead a team researching the production of cortisone, which was used to fight a range of ailments and had earned its discoverer, Edward Kendall, a Nobel Prize. As a secondary project, the team was also looking at producing estradiol, a sex hormone instrumental in reproductive functioning. It was while carrying out this research in 1951 that Djerassi accidentally synthesised a compound, 19-norprogesterone, which was very similar in structure to Marker's progesterone but considerably more powerful, including in its ability to stem ovulation.

In its early days the compound was only able to enter the body via injection, but further development meant that it could be taken by mouth. The oral contraceptive opened up a world of new opportunities for women around the globe and in the process made a fortune for Syntex, a company born out of a scheme to profit from the pharmacological properties of yams. As for Djerassi, he continued his scientific work and also carved out a successful career as a novelist and playwright.

It's a dog's life

Before the discovery of insulin, the prognosis for diabetes sufferers wasn't good. Dietary regulation could prolong life, but fatality from the illness was the norm. When insulin was discovered in the early 1920s, diabetes became eminently manageable and no longer a death sentence. The story of this discovery began in Europe towards the end of the previous century with, rather unpromisingly, the observation of some particularly potent dog wee.

In 1889 Oskar Minkowski and Joseph von Mering were working at the University of Strasbourg on the links between pancreatic function and digestion. In the course of their research they removed the pancreas from a dog they were studying. A short while later a lab assistant drew their attention to flies gathering around a pool of the normally house-trained dog's urine. Thankfully, the scientists suppressed what must have been a strong urge to give the lab dog a swift kick and call in the cleaners. Instead they tested the urine and found out that the flies were attracted by the presence of sugar, a sure sign of diabetes. So it was that they established a firm link between the disease and the pancreas.

However, the credit for uncovering an effective treatment fell to two University of Toronto scientists, Frederick Banting and Charles Best, working in the lab of Professor John J.R. MacLeod in 1921. In humble quarters in the medical department there, the two men nurtured and experimented on a collection of dogs. Building on the research of Minkowski and von Mering, they tied off various of the dogs' pancreatic ducts to isolate those responsible for the secretions regulating blood sugar levels. One wonders if they imported a lamp post into the lab to help them obtain canine urine samples. Eventually they isolated insulin, the secreted hormone that keeps blood sugar balanced. After successful tests on the dogs, they then tried insulin on a classmate of Banting who was seriously ill with diabetes, reporting positive results. Within a year their work had entered into the mainstream and in 1923 they were awarded the Nobel Prize.

Minkowski was still alive to see a happy conclusion to the work he had begun over 30 years earlier. The death rate from diabetes fell from 64 per cent in 1914 to just over 1 per cent in 1957.

Dish of the day

Alexander Fleming was a biologist and pharmacologist and his discovery of penicillin in 1928 gave rise to the era of modern antibiotics. He was a highly talented researcher, but this particular discovery nonetheless relied on a rogue element finding its way into one of his experiments.

Fleming was born in Lochfield, Scotland in 1881 and took up his medical studies at St Mary's Hospital, London in 1901. A highly promising student, he seemed set for a career in surgery until his abilities as a rifleman intervened – the captain of the St Mary's rifle club didn't want to lose Fleming, and so secured him a berth in the research department, where he worked alongside Sir Almroth Wright, a leading name in the field of immunology.

Fleming remained at St Mary's until the First World War, when he served in field hospitals in France. He witnessed first-hand how many soldiers died from bacterial infections caused by their wounds, and how others died as the result of ineffective antiseptics that actually destroyed the immune system quicker than bacteria. He gave much consideration to this problem when he returned to St Mary's after the war.

In 1922 Fleming was studying some common cold bacteria in a Petri dish. He himself was suffering from the ailment and was very congested. At some point a tear had fallen from his eye and found its way into one of the dishes. He noted how over a day or so the tear seemed to destroy the surrounding bacteria. He realised that there must be something in the tear that acted as an antibiotic without causing harm to human tissue. This he called lysozyme, though its practical use was limited as it attacked only fairly mild germs.

Nonetheless, it was an experience that had many echoes in the work he carried out in September 1928 which resulted in the discovery of penicillin. He had prepared for investigation several Petri dishes of staphylococci bacteria, which can cause numerous diseases in humans and animals. Notorious for the rather haphazard conditions in his lab, when Fleming returned to the dishes a few days later, he noticed that one had its lid disturbed and that a mould was growing, some foreign agent having fallen into the uncovered dish. Just as when his tear had fallen, the mould seemed to contain something that was fighting off the bacteria. At first he had trouble isolating the active component in the mould, but he eventually identified it as being of the genus *Penicillium* and so called it penicillin.

Fleming published the results of this work in 1929 in the *British Journal of Experimental Pathology*. However, penicillin wasn't destined to be an overnight success. It wasn't easy to cultivate the mould and then isolate the penicillin in useful quantities. In addition, Fleming lacked evidence that it would last long enough inside the human body to prove really effective. He considered that if it had any future it was probably as a treatment for external wounds.

It fell to a research team at Oxford University, led by Ernst Chain and Howard Florey, to re-examine Fleming's findings. By 1940 they had proved its potential to work within the body and by 1942 had successfully tested it on a human. Under the shadow of the Second World War, they secured funding from the British and American governments to find a way to mass-produce it, a goal they had achieved by 1944. Fleming, Chain and Florey were jointly awarded the Nobel Prize in 1945.

Cleanliness is next to godliness

Dr Ignaz Semmelweis is considered the founding father of antisepsis for his following of basic sanitary procedures in hospitals. In an era when the existence of germs hadn't even been established, Semmelweis was responsible for instituting a regime of antiseptic cleansing for all his staff. He introduced the programme having spent many years desperately seeking an explanation for the high death rate on the maternity ward on which he worked. However, the answer came only with the tragic accidental death of one of his colleagues.

Semmelweis was born in 1818 in what is now the Hungarian capital of Budapest. When a young man he embarked on a law degree at the University of Vienna but changed career direction after a medic friend invited him to a public dissection. After qualifying as a doctor in Vienna in 1844, he chose to specialise in obstetrics.

In this period there was a very high fatality rate in Europe among new mothers as a result of puerperal fever (also called childbed fever), an infection of the placental site. Only tuberculosis killed more women of child-bearing age, and over half of patients who contracted it died. In Semmelweis's hospital there were two maternity clinics. Records showed that Clinic 2 had puerperal fever fatality rates of between 2 per cent in a good year and 8 per cent in a bad one. The rate in Clinic 1, though, was consistently higher, running at between 5.5 per cent and 16 per cent. The problem haunted Semmelweis, who spent years studying potential differences between the two clinics that might explain the huge discrepancy.

Unfortunately, the hospital's boss, one Dr Johannes Klein, didn't take kindly to Semmelweis's work, which had brought unwelcome attention on the hospital. Semmelweis was forced out of his job in 1846 but when his replacement left within a year, Semmelweis returned. In his absence, an esteemed colleague called Dr Jakob Kolletschka had died at just 43 years old. He had sliced his finger with a scalpel while dissecting a cadaver in front of students and the wound had become fatally infected. A firm link was made between matter from the cadaver and Kolletschka's infection, prompting a terrible realisation in Semmelweis.

He and a great many other of the obstetrics staff had been in the habit of studying dead bodies before going on their maternity rounds. With no knowledge of germs and how they spread, the staff didn't bother to wash their hands in between. It was the doctors who had been bringing death to the new mothers. After much experimentation, Semmelweis settled on a chloride of lime wash, which he insisted all doctors on the ward used. The results were immediate, with death rates falling from 11.4 per cent in 1846 to 1.2 per cent in 1847. But before the year was out, cross-contamination from a cancer patient to the maternity ward caused an upsurge in mortality, so Semmelweis ordered that all staff (and not just doctors) should take up his cleaning programme. In time he also realised that not just people but objects too should be subject to the regime.

Never confident in his writing ability, it was several years before the doctor put down his ideas on paper. Though many in the medical profession embraced his advice, many others tried to discredit him. With germ theory still far from established, Semmelweis lacked empirical evidence for his beliefs, and many doctors simply didn't want to consider that they might have been responsible for their own patients' deaths by a lack of hygiene. The struggle for acceptance took its toll on Semmelweis and he was sectioned by his own wife in 1865, shortly before dying of blood poisoning.

Up, up and away

One of the most important and high-profile drugs developed in recent decades is Viagra, a medication used for the treatment of impotence and erectile dysfunction. But sildenafil citrate, the generic name for the drug, wasn't created with this purpose in mind – it was initially developed as a treatment for angina.

In the 1990s the drug manufacturer Pfizer Inc. was looking for an improved treatment for angina, a condition characterised by severe chest pain and caused by a lack of blood supply to the heart. Much of the early research work into Viagra took place in Britain, and by the mid-1990s clinical trials were under way at the Morriston Hospital in Swansea. The initial results weren't encouraging; the drug seemed to be having little effect on the symptoms of angina.

However, some patients were noticing other distinct side-effects. It was hoped that the drug would prompt vasodilation (widening of blood vessels) in the arteries around the heart. It was, in fact, prompting vasodilation in the arteries of the penis, causing impromptu and long-lasting sexual arousal in men who had in some cases been impotent for years.

Pfizer was quick to see the potential of the drug and redirected the course of their Viagra development programme. Viagra was patented in 1996 and went on general sale two years later. While not the first treatment for impotence, it was the first effective oral medication to become available and was an instant worldwide hit. By 2001 it was racking up sales of over US$1 billion per year. The phrase 'happy accident' is often used in discussion of Viagra. It is indeed difficult to think of another chance discovery that will have brought so many smiles to so many faces.

Aspirin is another drug that was created for one purpose for which it was ineffective but then found to be good for treating other problems. In the late 19th century it was developed in the hope that it could be taken internally to fight bacterial infections. Alas, it didn't work on that front, but in the 1890s the firm Bayer marketed it as a means to relieve pain and fever. In more recent times it has also been identified as a valuable weapon against heart attacks.

CHAPTER 8

World of Sport

Despite rafts of tales of shock and surprise, the sporting world in reality has little scope for the truly unexpected. Most sporting occasions are tiresomely predictable, dominated by characters born with innate talents honed by long periods of concentrated practice. Even those instances described as 'upsets' usually have their roots in fairly mundane circumstances; a favourite has a bad day or someone manages to raise their game for a one-off contest. Much rarer is to find a set of entirely unpredictable circumstances that allow for a team or individual to reach goals they could never reasonably have dreamed of.

Anyone for tennis?

In truth, the Irish aren't renowned as a nation of tennis players. So it comes as something of a surprise to find that it was Irishman John Pius Boland who claimed not only the men's singles title but, for good measure, the doubles too at the first modern Olympic Games.

The original Olympics were held in Athens in the 8th

century BC but were resurrected in 1896, with Athens again their home. Boland was something of an intellectual, an Oxford graduate with a taste for Greek mythology. In 1894 he was responsible for inviting one Thrasyvoalos Manaos to speak at the Oxford Union on the subject of the Olympic Revival movement. The two became tight friends and Manaos extracted a promise that Boland would visit him in Greece to join in the Olympic celebrations.

So Boland rolled into Athens in Easter 1896, looking forward to spectating at the Games. However, Manaos was on the organising committee of the Games and, after he saw the Irishman in a friendly match of tennis, suggested he might want to join the field, which was a little on the light side. Using his influence, Manaos made sure the late entrant was put into the competition.

Playing apparently effortless tennis (despite donning decidedly unergonomic leather-soled shoes with heels), Boland defeated an Egyptian, Dionysios Kasdaglis, in the singles final. He then began the doubles campaign alongside Friedrich Traun, a German whom he had rather unsportingly defeated in the first round of the singles. Boland and Traun defeated Demetrios Petrokokkinos of Greece and Kasdaglis (again) in the final. Kasdaglis, especially, must have wished Boland had stayed in Ireland.

Our accidental conquering hero returned home to carve out a career in politics, winning a seat in the British parliament and campaigning for Irish independence. As such, it would have pleased him that, although his medals were initially credited to the British team, he was subsequently recognised in the official histories as Ireland's first Olympic champion.

Danish back in

It's not unusual for apparent no-hopers to put in unexpectedly good showings at big international football tournaments – perhaps a berth in the quarter- or semi-finals followed by gallant defeat on penalties to one of the Old Guard. It's much rarer for a dark horse to come out of nowhere and win the whole thing. But that's exactly what Denmark did at the 1992 European Championships. Not bad for a tournament that should never have included them.

In the finals, Denmark were drawn in what looked like an insurmountably difficult group, alongside hosts Sweden and perennial 'big guns' France and England. Denmark had a fairly unremarkable squad, save for two out-and-out world-class players in goalkeeper Peter Schmeichel and tricksy midfielder Brian Laudrup.

After an opening draw with England and then a loss to Sweden, things looked predictably bleak. Then an unexpected 2–1 win against France propelled them into the semi-finals. Already over-achieving, they now faced the Netherlands, defending champions boasting a star-studded team. At this stage Denmark played the traditional plucky underdog role, drawing 2–2 to take the tie to penalties. Forgetting the script, they then won the shoot-out. Bring on the final against reigning world champions, Germany. A goal in each half (by the unheralded duo of John Jensen and Kim Vilfort) secured Denmark the trophy. It was a victory with which no one could argue.

Yet the fact was that Denmark had failed to even qualify for Euro '92. Their qualification campaign had been something of a catastrophe, not least because of a serious falling out between the coach, Richard Møller Nielsen, and his star player, Michael Laudrup (brother of Brian), which saw Laudrup suspend his international career. Denmark finished second in their group behind Yugoslavia and were out.

The story goes that as the finals were about to get under way in June 1992, the Danish players were tanning themselves on an assortment of beaches around the world while their manager was preparing to overhaul his kitchen. But Yugoslavia's complex politics had descended into an all-out civil war that would see the country's eventual dissolution. With the United Nations having implemented sanctions against it, Yugoslavia was banned from participating in UEFA's European Championship. So it was that the Danish Football Association was left to take its place and hurriedly reassemble their squad, who stepped out in their first match in hope rather than expectation.

As one corner of Europe collapsed into brutality, so another corner bore witness to one of football's most romantic stories.

Slow and steady wins the race

Foinavon has gone down in Grand National folklore as the 100/1 outsider who won at a canter in 1967. It was no accident that he had such long odds, and indeed he was lagging at the back of the field as the 23rd jump loomed into view. But it was the fact that he found himself so far behind his opponents that allowed him to dodge the utter chaos that erupted at that fence and trace a path to unlikely victory.

Foinavon was once owned by the Duchess of Westminster, but his basic dislike of jumping over hurdles quickly became apparent and he was shipped on. He was then trained at John Kempton's yard, where he managed a few victories and even raced in the Cheltenham Gold Cup. But no one thought he stood a chance in the National.

Kempton was not only Foinavon's trainer but usually rode him in races too. However, he was unable to make the required weight at Aintree on the day of the National, so instead went to Worcester to take another ride. That stroke of (mis)fortune allowed the unassuming John Buckingham to take his place and race in his first National, straight into the annals of sporting legend.

It was another horse called Popham Down to whom Foinavon owes his fame. Popham Down had unseated his rider at the first fence, but, having got a taste for the action, continued to hurtle around the course. Until the 23rd, that is. Along with a couple of other riderless chums, he chose not to jump that fence but instead to run up and down its length. That caused the leading jockey-carrying horses to consider their options, and they all chose either to refuse or else throw their humans. It was a trend picked up by every horse left in the field bar one: Foinavon. Going slowly enough to take in exactly what was going on ahead, he glided to the outside of the fence and jumped safely.

A further seventeen horses were finally persuaded to jump too, but by then Foinavon was a very decent distance ahead. Two of the much fancied runners, Red Alligator and Honey End, for a while threatened to close the gap, but they expended so much energy catching him up that they were never really in contention. At the line, Honey End finished a good way behind Foinavon, who was destined to enjoy the sweetest end of all.

Foinavon raced at the following year's National and was well in among them until he was brought down by a water jump. His name has lived on at Aintree, though, with fence number seven named after him. Meanwhile, Kempton, the man who might have been a Grand National legend, watched events unfold on television having earlier run a winner of his own at Worcester.

Skating on thin ice

It would be pleasing to think that Australian speed skater Steven Bradbury had made a study of Foinavon's tactics before doing the human equivalent at the 2002 Salt Lake City Winter Olympics. Coming from a country not renowned for its winter sport prowess, Bradbury was a solid skater who managed a bronze medal at the Lillehammer Olympics in 1994. Yet he came into the 1,000m in 2002, at his third Olympics, with little hope of a medal.

Having made it safely through the opening round, he looked to have been skated out of contention in the quarter-finals, coming third with only two racers progressing. However, when his competitor, Marc Gagnon, was disqualified, Bradbury found himself back in the semi-final line-up. Presumably practising his tactics for the final, Bradbury was a distant fifth in the next round when three of his competitors crashed out. Finishing second, he had made it through to the Olympic final.

His strategy now finely honed, Bradbury (the oldest man on the start-line) resumed his familiar position at the back of the field. A couple of fallers and he would be in a medal position. But as the race neared its end, things weren't looking promising – Apolo Ohno, Ahn Hyun-Soo, Li Jiajun and Mathieu Turcotte were all ahead of him coming into the final bend. Then from nowhere, Li Jiajun stumbled and a huge pile-up ensued, removing all four of his opponents from contention. Bradbury drifted around the heap of bodies, scooted over the line and claimed Australia's first-ever Winter gold.

Bradbury candidly acknowledged his tactics in a post-race interview, saying: 'There was no point in getting there and mixing it up because I was going to be in last place anyway. So I figured I might as well stay out of the way and be in last place and hope that some people get tangled up.'

Few begrudged him his victory after a long career in

which he had to overcome a string of serious injuries. His achievement was even commemorated on a postage stamp, but no greater glory can there be for an Australian (not even an Olympic gold) than to find that your name has become part of the vernacular. In the subsequent years, 'to do a Bradbury' has become shorthand for someone coming from the back of the field to unexpectedly take the prize. As the great man himself was to comment on his moment of glory: 'God smiles on you some days and this is my day.'

The Real deal

Julio Iglesias has had a remarkable musical career in which he has sold over 300 million albums and has no doubt provided the soundtrack to just as many holiday romances. Were it not for a devastating car accident, though, it's likely that he would be associated not with the No. 1 position in the music charts but with the No. 1 shirt of Real Madrid.

Few other clubs can match the successes of Real, but the 1950s and 60s were a period of extraordinary glory even by their standards. They won five consecutive European Cups between 1956 and 1960 and had enjoyed another three final appearances by 1966. For a boyhood fan, there could be nothing more exciting than to be part of the club.

That was the situation in which a young Julio found himself at the beginning of the 1960s. Blessed with dashing good looks, he was goalkeeper for the youth team of the world's greatest side. If that were not enough, he was starting to hint at the breadth of his talents by studying law on the side too. Life must indeed have seemed too good to be true. Then in September 1963 it all fell apart.

A car crash left Julio with massive injuries to his neck and spinal column. He could forget about football – his doctors weren't even sure that he would walk again. As part of his gruelling recovery programme, it was suggested that learning the guitar might improve his manual dexterity. He quickly discovered a previously unknown aptitude for music. He was eventually well enough to resume his academic studies but gave them up in 1968, when he triumphed at the Benidorm International Song Festival, a competition that secured his future in the music world.

Famed for his smooth delivery of romantic ballads, his records have sold consistently across five decades. In 2001 he finally completed the law degree he had put on hold in favour of music, fulfilling a promise made to his father. Yet despite his global success, Julio was unable to replicate Real's form in European competition. He came a distant fourth to Ireland's Dana in the 1970 Eurovision Song Contest.

Police brutality

Torquay isn't one of English football's glamour clubs. Nonetheless, the Gulls, as they are known, joined the Football League in 1927 and had a proud history of never having dropped out of it as they went into the final game of the 1986–87 season. On that particular day they were third from bottom of the then fourth (and lowest) division. Torquay, Burnley and Lincoln City were separated by just two points, and one of them was destined to crash into non-league football by the end of the day.

Torquay faced Crewe Alexandra, who fielded a talented future captain of England, David Platt. By half-time Torquay were two goals down. A goal early in the second half gave them a ray of hope, but wave after wave of attack was repelled by Crewe. Elsewhere, Burnley were winning and seemed destined for safety. Lincoln were losing but started the day a point ahead of Torquay, so it was the Gulls who seemed doomed.

There were just minutes of normal time remaining when four new legs came onto the pitch and made all the difference. Bryn was a police dog charged with keeping an eye on the crowds at Torquay's match. As he paraded up and down the touchline, his attention was drawn to the activities of the Gulls' defender, Jim McNichol. It would seem that Bryn had got it into his head that the big centre-half was making a beeline for the dog's handler so, in a desperate bid to avert disaster, Bryn courageously sprinted into the match action and sank his canines into McNichol's thigh.

After some wrangling, the intrepid hound was eventually removed from the player, but the unfortunate McNichol remained in some discomfort. The match was halted to allow him to receive treatment and the referee prepared to play four minutes of added time to make up the difference. The rhythm of the match had been crucially disrupted and, as the fourth added minute approached its end, Gulls' striker Paul Dobson forced home the goal that saved Torquay and sent Lincoln out of the league. Despite attacking one of their key players, Bryn became an immediate hero on the English Riviera.

Dia by name, dire by nature

Ali Dia, regularly named the worst player ever to play top-flight football, has a story that relies on two huge strokes of almost unbelievable luck: the failure of a Premiership football club to do the most cursory bit of research, and then a spell of bad weather. Dia's career at the highest level may have lasted little over twenty minutes, but it did earn him a place in football folklore.

As the 1996–97 season swung into action, Ali Dia, a Senegalese national in his early 30s, was probably dreaming of what might have been and reflecting on his most recent stint at the English semi-professional club, Blyth Spartans. That had come after spells amid the lower rungs of French and German football and a series of failed attempts to get into the English lower leagues.

Then Dia's agent conjured up a scheme that even in his wildest dreams he must have believed was doomed. The plan was simple to the point of stupidity. He would ring Premier League managers pretending to be George Weah (then World Player of the Year) and claim that Dia was his prodigiously talented cousin. A false career history was also devised, including a long stint with continental giants Paris St Germain and thirteen international caps. The agent rang Graeme Souness, then manager of Southampton, who had made his name as the no-nonsense Scottish enforcer in the great Liverpool teams of the 1970s and 80s. Somehow, and quite how has never fully been explained, he was completely taken in and a deal was rushed through. Dia was in the big league!

He was pencilled in to play a reserve game against Arsenal, during which his complete inadequacy at that level would surely have come to light. However, torrential rain saw the match postponed. Instead he was thrust straight into the first team squad for the game against Leeds on 23 November 1996. After half an hour Matthew Le Tissier, arguably the most naturally gifted player of his generation, was injured and Dia was sent on in his place. Twenty-two minutes later Dia himself was substituted after a cameo described by Le Tissier as 'embarrassing to watch'.

The Southampton physio claims that Dia came in for some treatment on a minor knock the following day, but no more was ever heard from the player at Southampton. His work done, he clearly knew it was time to leave. He later turned up in the colours of non-league Gateshead from where, after an encouraging debut goal, he was released after eight days.

Ultimately, no serious harm was done and the Southampton faithful even had a new chant to sing: 'Ali Dia, he's a liar.' That such a preposterous scam was pulled off so effectively (until actually having to play football was unnecessarily dragged into the equation) suggests that greater forces must surely have been at work.

Audience participation

Steve Davies, a 27-year-old West Ham fan, probably had even less hope than Ali Dia of making a name for himself in football's top tiers. However, in a pre-season friendly at Oxford in 1994 he was given the opportunity to prove himself by West Ham assistant manager, Harry Redknapp. During a hugely successful managerial career, Redknapp has won a reputation for signing talent at rock-bottom prices. Davies, though, must be the only player Redknapp has played in his team who had to buy his own ticket for the game.

Davies probably had West Ham running through his veins. What is beyond dispute is that the team's name was tattooed across his neck. Feeling that perhaps the Hammers weren't giving their absolute all, he set about discreetly communicating his concerns to the players. Lee Chapman, the Hammers' striker, was coming in for some particularly fruity advice when something in Redknapp snapped. He turned to Davies and demanded of him whether he could back up his abuse with a performance on the pitch. Despite having given up park football six years earlier, Davies was up for the challenge.

Plucked from the terraces, he was sent off to the dressing

rooms in company with a member of the West Ham staff and returned ten minutes later in a fresh Hammers' strip, ready to mix it with his highly-paid new colleagues. Despite being somewhat out of his league, Redknapp recalled that he did manage to contribute a goal to the cause. Alas, it wasn't enough to secure a longer deal with Big 'Arry, who took over as first team manager a month later.

At the time of the game, the World Cup was being played in the United States. As Redknapp threw Davies into the thick of the action, an Oxford journalist wandered over to ask him who the new player was. 'Haven't you been watching the World Cup?' asked a deadpan Harry. 'That's the great Bulgarian, Tittyshev!'

CHAPTER 9

Musical High Notes

I t can be very hard to pinpoint why one musician becomes a superstar while another of seemingly comparable talents never makes it beyond the recognition of a select few. Similarly, what is the magic ingredient that propels certain songs into the collective consciousness while others fade into nothingness? The answer may well rest with the guiding hand of serendipity. John Quincy Adams, the sixth president of the United States of America, was not (to my knowledge) a gifted musician but he did have a finely tuned sense of serendipity's unseen influence. He once commented that his own life had been 'marked by great and signal success which I neither aimed at nor anticipated'.

Dreaming of 'Yesterday'

The melancholic 'Yesterday' by The Beatles was released in 1965 and, despite sounding unlike anything else the band had recorded to that point, sold in its millions. Over time it has entered the *Guinness Book of Records* as the most covered song of all time, with over 3,000 different recordings in existence.

A simple tune with engagingly doleful lyrics, it's the type of song that most composers can only dream of. Paul McCartney, the Beatle responsible for it, had the good fortune to awake from a dream with the tune fully formed in his mind.

McCartney was staying in London at the time in the attic of the Wimpole Street family home of his then girlfriend, Jane Asher. McCartney recalled waking one morning from a dream featuring the playing of a string ensemble. Fortunately, his room was equipped with an upright piano, so McCartney sprang from his bed and tried to reproduce the melody he had been listening to. It came together with remarkable ease, and for a time Paul suspected that he couldn't have actually 'written' the piece because it was so different from his usual output. Terrified that he had subconsciously picked up the tune elsewhere and that he would be accused of plagiarism, he spent weeks playing the tune to friends in the music industry until he was convinced of its originality.

At this stage the tune didn't yet have any words, and was known by the title 'Scrambled Eggs'. After the instantaneous creation of the tune, it was several months before the lyrics were completed, when Paul was on holiday in Portugal. Even when complete, it seems 'Yesterday' wasn't an immediate favourite of the other Beatles, and it wasn't released as a single in the UK until 1976, when it reached only No. 8. However, it went to No. 1 in the States in 1965 and Matt Monro took a cover version into the UK top ten later in the year. The song's unprecedented recording history has seen acts as diverse as Bob Dylan, Liberace, Placido Domingo and Boyz II Men all attempt to stamp their mark on it. In 1999 listeners to BBC Radio 2 voted it the best song of the 20th century.

S-Club sandwich

Born in 1978, at the age of nineteen Rachel Stevens became 'the glamorous one' in the manufactured pop band, S Club 7. It was the realisation of a dream that Stevens had harboured since the age of twelve, when she went to see Kylie Minogue in concert. And it was a chance lunch date that made it all possible.

When she was fifteen, Stevens won a magazine competition to find a new model. She had a passion for fashion and decided she would make it her career. When she was old enough she began studying at the London School of Fashion and worked in public relations.

In 1997 she arranged to meet her brother for lunch one day in the canteen of a record company where he was working at the time. It so happened that also lunching there were two A&R men who worked for the pop impresario, Simon Fuller. Fuller had managed the Spice Girls during their glory days and, having split with them, formed a plan to create the perfect pop group, consisting of four girls and three boys. He had a very clear idea of the look that he wanted, and his A&R men at the canteen saw how Rachel might just fit the bill.

They approached her to ask if she could sing. She told them that she could, and within days Fuller was in possession of a demo tape. He invited her to audition for the band (the only S-Clubber honoured in this way) and soon enough she had beaten off competition from 10,000 other hopefuls to make the final line-up.

The band was launched via their own television series and went on to have huge success, selling over 13 million albums. Stevens went on to have a successful solo career and won renewed fame in 2008 when she received some of the highest scores ever seen in the television dance contest, Strictly Come Dancing. It's not known what she ordered for lunch on that fateful day but we may speculate that it was a jammy sandwich!

From bard to verse

Sheryl Crow had a slow-burning career which erupted into super-stardom with the release of the multi-million-selling *Tuesday Night Music Club* album in the mid-1990s. The album itself garnered only limited attention until the release of the single, 'All I Wanna Do'. It was a song that Crow had struggled to complete until her producer stumbled across a little-known volume of poetry in a second-hand bookshop. A discovery that changed the lives of not only Crow but the poet, Wyn Cooper, too.

Crow was a one-time elementary school teacher who carved out a career working on advertising jingles. In the late

1980s she was a backing singer for Michael Jackson on his Bad world tour. Crow was scheduled to release a solo album in 1992 but it never appeared. She then began working with a group of musicians known as the Tuesday Music Club, who would eventually become immortalised in the title of her album.

Wyn Cooper, meanwhile, was a university lecturer and poet, whose first volume, *The Country of Here Below*, was written while he was a postgraduate student. It was published in 1987 in a print-run of 500. It so happened that by 1992 one of these copies had ended up on the shelves of Cliff's Books in Pasadena, California – just around the corner from the studio where Sheryl and her band were working on her album.

Sheryl had one particularly great track but no one could come up with lyrics for it. During a break in proceedings, her producer, Bill Bottrell, popped round the corner to Cliff's and bought a stack of books that included Cooper's opus. A while later, he and Crow were thumbing through the pages when a poem called 'Fun' caught their eye. Crow realised that, with a few adaptations, it would fit her tune perfectly.

The song became 'All I Wanna Do' and was an international smash hit when it was released in the spring of 1994. When Crow approached Cooper for permission to use his words, he was so delighted that he almost agreed to waive royalties, but ultimately he earned enough from the song that he could turn his attentions to poetry full-time. Crow went on to receive three Grammy Awards in 1995. Bolstered by the attention, *The Country of Here Below* went into several new editions and Cooper continues to contribute lyrics to numerous musicians around the world.

Strait to the point

Brothers in Arms was one of the iconic albums of the 1980s, propelling Dire Straits to international superstardom as it topped the charts in 24 countries, including the UK and US. Its centrepiece and lead single was 'Money for Nothing'. Accompanied by a computer-animated video that was perfect for the MTV generation, its controversial lyrics parodied the instant consumer society of the period. 'Money for nothing and chicks for free' were very much the order of the day, at least in the world depicted on music television.

When the band released the track in 1985 it seemed they had come up with a minor masterpiece of social satire. In fact, they owed a very great deal of it to a worker whom their lead singer and guitarist (and former college lecturer), Mark Knopfler, had stumbled across in a store supplying kitchens and assorted electronic goods.

In an interview conducted in 1985, Knopfler admitted that the song's 'lead character' was this rather unreconstructed fellow he had spied on at the shop through a gap in a stack of microwaves. 'I wrote the song when I was actually in the store,' Knopfler said. 'I wanted to use a lot of the language that the real guy actually used when I heard him, because it was more real.'

Whether that gentleman knew that his observations on microwave ovens, custom kitchen deliveries, refrigerators and colour TVs would be turned into four-and-a-half minutes of stadium rock perfection isn't known. More definite is that Knopfler recognised that the workman's growled 'That ain't workin'' was pure lyrical gold.

Band of brothers

Love them or otherwise, Oasis livened up British music with a rush of exciting, straightforward rock'n'roll in the 1990s. The trials and tribulations between Liam and Noel, the Gallagher brothers who form the backbone of the band, are well documented. Yet should Noel have succeeded in passing an audition for a rival Mancunian band in the late 1980s, in all likelihood Oasis would never have got further than practices in Liam's bedroom.

In May 1988 Noel had gone to a concert by legendary 'Madchester' band, the Stone Roses. There he got into conversation with Graham Lambert, who played guitar for the Inspiral Carpets, another Manchester band who were on the verge of the big time. Noel became something of a regular at Inspirals concerts and when their singer, Steve Holt, quit the band, Noel was brought in to audition as his replacement. The band decided against taking him on, but they liked his attitude and employed him as a roadie.

In 1991 Noel came home after an American tour with the Inspirals and found that his little brother, Liam, was singing with a new local band, The Rain. When Noel went to see one of their gigs, he wasn't impressed but agreed to join if he could steer the band's direction and be the main songwriter. The Inspirals were to play one final pivotal role in the Oasis story, as it's often related that The Rain renamed themselves after a venue, the Oasis in Swindon, that appeared on an Inspirals tour poster that hung in the Gallaghers' bedroom.

The band's mix of great hooks and optimistic lyrics, contrasting against the pessimism of grunge that had marked the early 1990s music scene, quickly won a strong following. Alan McGee saw them play in Glasgow in 1993 and signed them on the spot. Their debut album, *Definitely Maybe*, was at the time the fastest-selling debut Britain had ever seen. Its follow-up, (*What's the Story*) *Morning Glory?*, established them as Britpop superstars. Today they are a British institution. While the Inspirals retain their own cult following, Noel is unlikely to regret the day he failed to become their singer.

Cabbages! Cabbages! One for a tenor!

Etienne Lainez was one of the stars of the Paris Opéra in the latter part of the 18th century and the beginning of the 19th. Yet his background never suggested that he would end up in such exalted company. As a boy growing up in Paris, he hawked around whatever his father was able to produce on the family's small plot of land. It was in this role, distinctly unstarry, that he got a remarkably lucky break.

Lainez was born in 1753 in Vaugirard, France. His father

was a lowly market-gardener and Etienne himself was often to be found selling fruit and vegetables in the Paris markets. Fighting to be heard among his market rivals, the teenage Etienne was bellowing 'Cabbages!' at the top of his voice on one particular day. In earshot happened to be Pierre-Montan Berton, Director of the Paris Opéra, who noticed a beguiling musicality in the young man's voice. Berton arranged singing lessons for his new protégé and in 1770 Etienne was auditioned at the Opéra.

The following year he entered the Opéra's school of singing and declamation. In 1773 he debuted at the Royal Academy of Music. He bided his time playing a series of smaller roles but got his next big break when he was required to stand in for Joseph Legros, one of the stars of the Opéra, in Alceste in 1776. When Legros retired in 1783, Lainez replaced him as the company's lead tenor. Despite being a royalist, he navigated his way safely through the French Revolution and was a big hit with Napoleon.

During his 40+-year career Lainez created over 50 roles and, with Legros safely out of the way, topped the bill at the Opéra on no fewer than eighteen occasions. His last years saw him in poor health and he was the subject of a benefit concert in 1810 but, keen to stay in the limelight as long as possible, carried on for a further two years until retiring in 1812. He then took over the management of the Lyon Opéra but had obviously forgotten the hard business lessons of the Paris vegetable market, for he soon found himself in serious debt. A return to Paris for another shot at the big time lasted less than one performance and he finished his days as a teacher in Marseille.

The composer's mews

An artist's inspiration may spring from the most unexpected sources and for the Neapolitan classical composer, Giuseppe Domenico Scarlatti, it arrived in the shape of his cat, Pulcinella.

Scarlatti was something of a musical prodigy. Born in 1685, by the time he was sixteen he was a musician at the Chapel Royal, and he soon moved to Rome to study with the finest musicians the country had to offer. By the time he was *maestro di cappella* at St Peter's Basilica in the Vatican, Scarlatti had established his reputation as a harpsichord player of unrivalled talent (with the possible exception of his friend, Handel) and a composer of note.

Scarlatti travelled widely and had extended stays in England, Portugal and Spain, where he was a guest of the Royal Court. He settled in Madrid in 1733 and remained there until his death 24 years later. It was during this period that Pulcinella came into his life. Pulcinella seems to have been an early exponent of jazz, often parading up and down the keyboard of her master's harpsichord, dabbing at certain notes every now and then. One particularly striking riff entered Scarlatti's consciousness and he set out to reproduce it exactly. It would become a dominant motif in his *Fugue in G minor, KK. 30.*

Possibly unwilling to share the glory with his befurred, musical-experimentalist companion, Scarlatti didn't publicly recognise the contribution of his cat. However, word evidently got out and the name *Cat's Fugue* was used in concert programme notes from the 19th century onwards.

Pulcinella wasn't the only fleet-pawed feline to inspire a composition. Chopin's efforts to reproduce the effect of his cat prancing up a piano keyboard were captured in his *Waltz No. 3 in F major*, also called *The Cat's Waltz*.

Church music

Charlotte Church has world album sales in excess of ten million and, by the time she turned 21, had navigated her career through classical and pop music, had embarked on a television career, was one half of the most famous couple in Wales (alongside rugby international, Gavin Henson), and was a mother to boot. Not surprisingly, her rise to stardom began very young, and it came as the result of what was meant to be her aunt's crack at fame.

In 1998 Charlotte's Aunty Caroline, a cabaret singer, had bagged herself a spot on a television talent show hosted by Jonathan Ross called *The Big, Big Talent Show*. One of the features of the programme was that each turn was introduced by a friend or family member. In the case of Caroline, it was her little niece who would provide the introduction. It so happened that the producers had come into possession of a tape of another television show, a quiz called *Talking Telephone*

Numbers, which had been broadcast a few months earlier. It featured Charlotte singing a few lines of the song 'Pie Jesu' down a phone line. Suitably impressed, the producers decided she should perform a few bars when introducing her aunt.

Ross briefly interviewed his eleven-year-old guest, establishing that she was a keen opera fan and that she would be happy to give the audience a burst 'as soon as I get a C off the orchestra'. From this small girl from South Wales came a huge, rich voice and the audience loved it. A few minutes later, out came Caroline for her turn, clad in classic rock chick garb and herself blessed with a booming voice. However, she didn't win the show and it was her niece's performance that stayed in everyone's mind

Within weeks of her TV debut, Charlotte had been booked for appearances at the Royal Albert Hall and the London Palladium. She had also been spotted by an entertainment impresario, Jonathan Shalit, who took her on as a client and had soon negotiated a recording deal with Sony BMG. Her debut album, *Voice of an Angel*, appeared before the year was out and traded on her aura of innocence. It saw her become the youngest person ever to top the classical charts and sold millions worldwide. She performed live in front of some of the world's most famous names, including Pope John Paul II, Bill Clinton and the Queen. In 2002, at the age of sixteen, she released her greatest hits album before moving away from classical and sacred music into more mainstream pop. She then began to host her own chat show. So it has been that, in an age of growing secularism, this Church of Wales has managed to win millions of believers.

Happily Eva after?

Little Eva burst onto the music scene in 1962, famously taking 'The Locomotion' to the top of the charts. Her chance at stardom came when she picked up one of the most fortunate babysitting gigs in history.

Eva Narcissus Boyd was born in 1943 in Belhaven, North Carolina, one of thirteen children. Among her relatives was an aunt, also called Eva. She was, naturally, Big Eva while Eva Narcissus became Little Eva. Brought up in a gospel singing tradition, she honed the powerful vocal skills that would serve her so well.

She moved to New York at the beginning of the 1960s, working as a maid. There she met Earl-Jean McCrae, a member of a vocal group called The Cookies. They were strongly associated with the Brill Building in New York, a focal point for various labels and music publishers responsible for a popular strain of 50s and 60s music that became known as the Brill Building Sound. Among the Brill Building's finest songwriting partnerships was a couple, Carole King and Gerry Goffin, who had made their name with 'Will You Love Me Tomorrow' for The Shirelles. Eva was doing some session work with The Cookies but to keep up her income she started babysitting King and Goffin's child for a princely $35 a week.

One day King came home to find the babysitter singing her own version of a song King had written for an established star, Dee Dee Sharp, and King asked Eva to provide backing vocals on the single. But her real break came with another song that King was in the process of working on for Sharp. It was 'The Locomotion'. King asked Eva to record a demo of the song to take to the record company. As soon as she heard Eva's version, she knew nobody would do it better and persuaded Dimension Records to release it as a Little Eva single in June 1962. Eva added her own unforgettable choreography and shot to No. 1 in the charts, beating Sharp's own effort, 'Gravy (For My Mashed Potatoes)'.

Eva had a handful more hits of her own, including 'Keep Your Hands Off My Baby', 'Let's Turkey Trot' and 'Old Smokey Locomotion', as well as with other artists, notably The Cookies and an uncredited appearance on Big Dee Irwin's 'Swingin' on a Star'. She was even the subject of a tribute song, 'Little Eva' by The Locomotions. Sadly for Eva, though, music tastes moved rapidly during the 1960s and, having been paid a salary rather than royalties during her peak, she had relatively little money. Her star shone brightly but only briefly and by the 1970s she was ready to retire from an industry that had rather tired of her.

Nonetheless, her name stayed on people's minds. Her version of 'The Locomotion' was a hit again in the UK in 1972 and was famously covered by Grand Funk Railroad and Kylie Minogue in later years. Little Eva began to tour again in the 1990s, buoyed by a wave of retro nostalgia. She died in 2003 after a long fight with cancer.

Timely success

For many music fans, rock'n'roll began in earnest with the release of 'Rock Around the Clock' by Bill Haley and His Comets. However, what is less well known is that the song was originally a B-side and it was only its fortuitous inclusion in a film that launched it on the path to eternal fame.

Bill Haley was born in 1925. Originally a country and western performer, Haley was quick to see the potential of adding in some rhythm and blues, thus combining the fundamental ingredients of rock'n'roll. In 1951 he released a cover of Jackie Brenston's 'Rocket 88' that has come to be regarded as the first bona fide rock'n'roll recording by a white artist. Nonetheless, rock'n'roll remained little more than an underground movement for the next few years.

In 1953 Haley and His Comets had a hit with 'Crazy, Man, Crazy', which led to their first deal with a major label, Decca Records. It was decided that their first single would be a song called 'Thirteen Women (and Only One Man in Town)'. On the B-side would be 'Rock Around the Clock', a two-minute, eight-second burst of high-octane rock'n'roll, written by Max Freedman and Jimmy De Knight and originally recorded by the novelty band, Sonny Dae and His Knights. In May 1954 'Thirteen Women' was released and became a minor hit. The B-side received little attention.

Two months later, Haley had a million-seller with 'Shake, Rattle and Roll'. The following year saw the release of a movie called *Blackboard Jungle*, the story of a teacher in a tough inner-city school. It starred Glenn Ford, the Hollywood actor who was married to Eleanor Powell and who had a young son, Peter. The film's producers wanted to include an authentically youthful soundtrack and so Ford borrowed some of his ten-year-old son's records for them to listen to. Among these was 'Thirteen Women', but it was the B-side that grabbed the producers' attention.

The film was a smash and 'Rock Around the Clock' in particular hit a chord with its youthful audience. It was re-released as an A-side, reaching the top of the charts in July 1955 and staying there for eight weeks. Suddenly rock'n'roll was out of the underground and into the mainstream. Haley and His Comets had a third million-seller the following year with 'See You Later, Alligator' before being somewhat overtaken by new acts, notably Elvis. But for a short while Bill Haley was the face of rock'n'roll. His most famous song got a new lease of life in the 1970s when it was used as the theme tune for the sitcom *Happy Days* and recharted after appearing on the soundtrack of the film *American Graffiti*. Haley died in 1981, a member of popular music aristocracy. Bill Haley and His Comets were estimated to have sold some 60 million records, with 'Rock Around the Clock' accounting for about 25 million of those.

CHAPTER 10

Great Escapes

In *The Lion, The Witch and the Wardrobe*, C.S. Lewis told the tale of a group of children who stumble into the magical land of Narnia by chance but find only the back of a wardrobe when they actively try to return there. It provides a classic lesson in how serendipity works. The entries in this chapter all deal with individuals in life-and-death situations who escaped the latter against all probability. Each escaped as the result of interventions that they neither sought nor anticipated.

The good luck buck

George Dixon was a good-looking young soldier on the Confederate side during America's Civil War. He had spent some time in Mobile, Alabama, where he had become engaged to one Queenie Bennett. Shortly before setting off to fight at the crucial Battle of Shiloh in 1862, she gave him a gold $20 piece that would save his life.

The battle was played out in the south-west part of Tennessee, and after initial successes by the Confederates, it was the Union forces of Ulysses S. Grant that ultimately won through. In the course of the drawn-out struggle, a Union bullet was fired with Dixon's name on it. It penetrated his trouser pocket but there encountered Queenie's coin, which enveloped itself around the deadly missile and prevented it from entering his leg.

Dixon knew he owed his life to the gold piece, and as soon as he got the opportunity he had it inscribed: 'Shiloh, April 6th 1862, My Life Preserver, G.E.D.' He carried it with him for the rest of his life, and the tale of how it saved him became one of the great legends of the Civil War.

In the period after the battle, while Dixon was recuperating, he became friends with William Alexander, one of the builders of a new submarine called *H.L. Hunley*. *Hunley* was launched in July 1863 with Lieutenant Dixon as its commander. It was then sent to Charleston, where it was hoped it might be able to end the crippling Union blockade of Charleston harbour. In February 1864 the 40-foot long *Hunley* sank the 1,240-ton *USS Housatonic* to become the world's first successful combat submarine. However, in the aftermath of the attack, *Hunley* was itself sunk with the loss of all its crew.

In 2000 the wreck of *Hunley* was rediscovered. The body of Dixon was found under the forward conning tower, his gold $20 – complete with bullet indentation and inscription – resting beside him.

Divine intervention

Frank Richards was a young British corporal with the 6th Liverpool Rifles during the First World War. Stationed in northern France, his battalion saw fierce fighting, during which Richards was shot. A bullet from an enemy rifle was on a direct path to his heart when the Bible he was carrying deflected it to safety.

The location of Richards' lucky escape isn't known today. He was certainly a participant in a surprise attack on the German line at Cambrai in November 1917. The battle started on the 21st of that month and Richards was reported missing on the 30th. He was then held as a prisoner of war at Munster in northern Germany before being released.

Whether or not he was wounded in this skirmish, we do know that he carried in his breast pocket a Bible published by the Young Men's Christian Association (YMCA) as part of their programme to provide as many troops as possible with a copy. The bullet that would surely have killed him instead went through the pages of his Bible and left him with nothing more serious than bruised ribs. Richards survived the rest of the war and died in 1966 at the age of 74. His wife donated the Bible, complete with bullet hole, to the National Museums of Liverpool.

He wasn't alone in having the Good Book to thank for his survival. Other documented cases include those of: Sam Houston at the Battle of Shiloh (again) in the American Civil War; William Wilson, a young American soldier fighting in France during the First World War; Patrick Caruso at

Iwo Jima in the Second World War; David Knapp in the Korean War; and Brendon Schweigart in Iraq in 2007.

Alive on the ocean wave

'Lucky Tower' is the name given to a legendary figure who was supposed to have survived not one shipwreck but three. He is said to have escaped the sinking of the *Titanic* in 1912, of the *Empress of Ireland* in 1914 and the *Lusitania* a year later. In subsequent decades much scepticism was heaped on the story, and indeed no one seemed too sure just who the miraculous Mr Tower was. However, research in recent years suggests that this particular urban myth may well be rooted in fact.

Firstly, we should probably dismiss the existence of a man named Tower. This seems to have come about after some rather lazy journalism. RMS *Lusitania*, built in Scotland, was one of Cunard's great ocean liners. In 1915 it was torpedoed by a German U-boat off the Kinsale coast of Ireland. It sank in less than twenty minutes, claiming the lives of 1,198 out of 1,959 passengers and crew. Among the survivors was one of the ship's firemen, a man called Frank Toner. In the Irish press reports that circulated in the days after the tragedy, it was he who was identified as the man who had survived three shipping disasters.

The White Star Line's RMS *Titanic* had, of course, sunk when it hit an iceberg on its maiden voyage from Southampton to New York in 1912. To this day it rates as the most infamous maritime disaster of them all, with over 1,500 people drowning in the catastrophe. RMS *Empress of Ireland* was owned by Canadian Pacific Steamships and met its end on the Saint Lawrence River after a collision with a Norwegian collier. Over 1,000 people perished. Yet neither of these vessels listed either a Tower or a Toner on their books. So what of the claims of the survivor from the *Lusitania*?

Extensive research by Senan Molony, an author and expert on these tragedies, has in recent years offered up some interesting theses. He has shown that there was one William Clark who worked as a stoker on *Titanic* and *Empress of Ireland*, surviving both wrecks. The chances of making it through even these two events were thin to say the least, yet local legend in his home town of Drogheda spoke of a third disaster too. Additionally, physical descriptions of Clark and Toner correspond in several key respects. Is it possible that Clark, not wishing to carry around a reputation as a bad omen for a ship, changed his identity for a stint on the *Lusitania*? The tale of 'Lucky Tower' may be improbable, but it's by no means implausible.

Harry's hat-trick

Henry 'Harry' Heth was a Confederate general in the US Civil War. It was he who instigated the famous Battle of Gettysburg in 1863 and it was at that engagement that he escaped the reaper's scythe when his oversized hat saved him from a bullet to the head.

Heth was born in Virginia in 1825. His future in the military didn't look overly rosy when he graduated from military academy at the bottom of his class. Nonetheless, once serving, he made steady progress and was soon promoted to captain. When civil war broke out in 1861, the old Virginian naturally joined the Confederate side

He performed bravely, if somewhat hot-headedly, as the war progressed and was promoted to major general in 1863 by Robert E. Lee, the Confederate commander who had taken Heth under his wing. Stationed in Pennsylvania, in the summer of 1863 Heth sent out a brigade on a mission to hunt down a supply of shoes rumoured to be in Gettysburg. The brigade, led by James Pettigrew, spotted some enemy soldiers and, in accordance with Lee's orders, backtracked to avoid a confrontation for which they were unprepared. Heth, though, decided to carry on through to Gettysburg and thus precipitated a battle with the Union cavalry of Brigadier General John Buford. As both sides were reinforced over the coming days, the Battle of Gettysburg turned into the single most bloody encounter of the whole war and proved to be a turning point that would ultimately see the defeat of the Confederacy.

However, for Heth, things might have been a lot worse. Shortly before the battle he got a newly requisitioned felt hat which was far too big for him. In order to keep it fixed on his head, he stuffed it with paper. In the heat of battle, Heth found himself in the enemy firing line. A Union bullet made straight for his head and penetrated his hat, but was deflected to safety by the tightly bound paper inside it. Though knocked unconscious, he made a complete recovery and was able to lead his forces for the remainder of the war until, alongside Lee, he surrendered in 1865.

Perhaps his lucky escape made Heth consider more carefully life's risks, because after the war he was employed in the insurance business.

Excess baggage

John Robertson was just sixteen when the Second World War broke out in 1939, and he soon signed up to join the RAF. He flew over 70 missions during the war, including one that culminated with the most unlikely of escapes following an incident of 'friendly fire'.

Robertson was a tail gunner in 108 Squadron. In April 1942 he was flying in a Vickers Wellington from Kibrit in Egypt to carry out a mission over Tripoli in Libya. It so happened that a US B-24 Liberator had been assigned a similar task and was flying the same path at an altitude above the Wellington. There was a lot of flak in the sky over the intended target and the scene was rather confused. Amid it all, none of the Wellington's crew noticed anything out of the ordinary with regard to their plane.

However, when they had completed the 300-mile journey back to Egypt, they saw the ground crew at the Kibrit airfield scattering as they landed. Why they weren't rushing over to greet the returning crewmen was something of a mystery – at least until Robertson and his comrades climbed out of their aircraft to discover a 250-lb bomb protruding from the tail fin, about three feet from Robertson's station. It emerged that the bomb had been dropped from the Liberator, miraculously lodging itself into the aircraft flying below it without exploding, or indeed attracting the attention of Robertson or any of his colleagues. The Wellington had then deposited its own missiles on its target before setting off for home, content with a job well done.

A team of bomb disposal experts took over proceedings, evacuating the area before carrying out a detailed exam-ination of the missile, which turned out to be in perfect working order. After the war, the much decorated Robertson chose a quieter life and opened a bookshop with his brother.

Hanging around

In February 1885 John Lee was facing the gallows, having been convicted of killing his employer. But on a traumatic day for the hangman, Lee survived three separate attempts to take his life. His sentence was subsequently commuted to 22 years in prison. After his release he won considerable fame and fortune as 'the man they couldn't hang'.

The strange story began with the gruesome murder of an 86-year-old woman, Emma Keyse, at Babbacombe Bay, Devon, in late 1884. She had been hacked to pieces before her home was set on fire. The finger of suspicion soon turned towards her employee, John Lee. With no apparent theft from her property, the motive seemed to have been ensuring the old spinster's silence on some subject. Lee was found guilty and sentenced to hang at Exeter Prison on 22 February 1885.

Lee was undoubtedly of dubious character and had served time in prison the previous year for theft. On the day he was to be hanged, a large crowd gathered in anticipation. The night of 21 February had been a cold and damp one, though, and it had an adverse effect on the gallows' drop mechanism. The time came for Lee to receive his punishment but when the executioner pulled the lever, nothing happened. A second go gave the same result, as did a third, despite the mechanism being tested and certified as working between each attempt.

Having beaten the hangman three times, Lee had his sentence commuted by the Home Secretary and he walked free in 1907, having spent over twenty years claiming he wasn't guilty of the crime. A minor celebrity, he sold his story to the press and travelled the country giving talks on his life. He even claimed that the night before his great escape he had dreamed that the trap-door would fail to open. In 1909 he remarried, but within two years he had left his wife and two children to fend for themselves in the poor house. He then fled to North America with a barmaid who he claimed was his wife. The rest of his life is somewhat shrouded in mystery, but it seems likely that he died in Milwaukee in 1945 of natural causes.

Remarkably, Lee wasn't the first man to have escaped

death in such a way. Back in 1803 in Australia, one Joseph Samuels was sentenced to hang after being found guilty of robbery and the murder of a policeman. Confessing to the first charge, he vehemently denied the second, claiming that his accomplice had been responsible for the death. Nonetheless, the day came in Sydney when Samuels found himself with the noose around his neck. Then at the crucial moment the rope broke and Samuels simply crashed to the ground, dazed but alive. A second attempt ended when the rope unravelled until Samuels was standing on the ground. The third go also failed when the rope snapped just above the convict's head. A later inspection showed it to be otherwise in good condition and quite capable of doing the job it was designed for. When news of the triple escape reached official ears, Samuels was given an immediate reprieve.

Cat-ching a ride

There are many tales of our feline friends getting into and then out of quite epic scrapes, several involving intercontinental travel. For instance, in 2006 a cat who came to be known as 'Chairman Miaow' somehow found her way into a crate of crockery at a dock in China and survived the subsequent journey to Kirby-in-Ashfield in Nottinghamshire. She lived on a diet of cardboard and condensation. But perhaps the luckiest explorer cat of them all was Colin's (or Colin's Cat to give her her full name), a feisty tortoiseshell from New Zealand.

Colin's' adventure happened in 2001 but her story began something like a decade earlier when she was abandoned at a tanker terminal at Port Taranaki in New Plymouth. There she was adopted by a kindly shipping manager called Colin Butler. With the charm and cunning typical of the average kitty, Colin's endeared herself to all the right people and worked out that by playing the shift system with its change-over of staff, she could guarantee an almost constant supply of food.

In 2001 her eternal quest for sustenance saw Colin's approach an engineer working on a tanker called *Tomawaka* which was passing through the port. She followed him on board, secured herself a good meal and then settled down for a post-prandial nap in the sailor's cabin. Alas, the vessel set sail before she got back to land. It was destined for South Korea.

Communications between the port and the tanker established what had happened, and Gordon Macpherson (who took over feline welfare duties after the original Colin had moved from the port) suggested they simply bring her back on the return voyage. However, the tanker was on its final voyage and was scheduled to be scrapped on its arrival back in Korea. Elaborate plans for a mid-ocean ship-to-ship transfer for the cat proved to be just too dangerous and impractical to attempt.

Macpherson thus decided that he would simply have to get to South Korea to pick up the stowaway and bring her home. Such was the international interest in the cat's tale that a cat food manufacturer agreed to pay for the considerable costs of the rescue mission. So Macpherson flew out to Yeosu for an emotional reunion and Colin's was even allowed to bypass the country's normally strict quarantine rules. She was given a seat next to her companion on the plane, and on her return to New Plymouth she was made an honorary ambassador 'in recognition of her involvement in the enhancement of international relations'.

She lived out the remainder of her life at the port, happily stalking seagulls and enjoying the benefits of a cat food sponsorship deal. Colin came back to see her too, while Macpherson noted that her unplanned Asian trip had left her 'older and wiser'.

Saving Grace

In 1928 Beatrice Lillie, one of the great stage stars of the day, was touring Canada in a Nöel Coward show called *This Year of Grace*. The highly professional Lillie uncharacteristically fluffed her words one night during a song, an error that inadvertently saved the life of several members of the show's chorus.

Beatrice Lillie was born Constance Munston in Canada in 1894. She moved to London in search of fame and fortune and in 1914 took to the West End stage, winning a reputation that saw her tagged 'the funniest woman in the world'. In 1920 she married one Robert Peel and within a few years had inherited the title of Lady Peel. In 1924 Beatrice returned to North America, winning much praise for her performances on Broadway and enticing some of the greatest writers of the day to work for her.

This Year of Grace had already triumphed in New York before going on an extensive North American tour. On this particular fateful night, it was playing in London, Ontario. One of its highlights was a thumping rendition of 'Rule Britannia', with Lillie backed by the full chorus. At the end of verse two they were to move centre stage, but on that evening in London, Lillie inexplicably rattled off the second verse twice, ensuring that the chorus remained stationed at the side of the stage.

The orchestra adjusted and managed to get the song back on track again, and the chorus was all primed to take up its rightful position. But just as they were about to do so, a huge arc light fell from the rig directly above the middle of the stage. Whoever had found themselves underneath it would have had little chance. As it was, no one was harmed and, with classic 'show must go on' spirit, Lillie hit the chorus as her colleagues shuffled on stage, hiding the wreckage.

CHAPTER 11

Inventions and Innovations (Part 2)

Here we have a further collection of life-changing creations that came about through happy and unexpected circumstance. Mark Twain, one of the great men of American literature, once remarked that '"Accident" was the greatest of all inventors'.

A cracking idea

The origins of glass aren't clear, but Pliny the Elder, the Roman writer who famously documented the eruption of Mount Vesuvius, claimed that its invention came about entirely by accident. It was his belief that Phoenician traders were once encamped on the shores of Palestine and used blocks of natron (carbonate of soda) that they had aboard ship as props for their cooking pots. The heat of their fires caused the carbonate of soda to melt and combine with the sand on the shore. When the sailors awoke the next morning, this mix had formed into molten glass. This occurrence is estimated to have happened some time around 4000 BC, although the first archaeological evidence of man-made glass are Egyptian bottles dating from around 1500 BC.

Our knowledge of the origins of safety glass is more certain. Edouard Benedictus was a French chemist (and notable artist) who, in 1903, smashed a glass flask in his lab. When he went to inspect the damage, he was surprised to see that the flask hadn't exploded into shards but, although it had shattered, had retained its original shape. Closer study showed that the glass was held together by a film that had formed on the inside of the flask. Checking back over what the flask had been filled with, he discovered that it was a solution of collodion. He realised that the solution must have evaporated out of the uncorked flask, leaving a residue on the interior.

Though intrigued, Benedictus didn't immediately follow up his discovery. However, over the course of a few months he read a series of distressing reports of car accidents in Paris. Many of the worst injuries, he noticed, were a result of flying glass. Realising that he might just have the perfect solution, he set about perfecting a manufacturing process for safety glass, which initially involved a letter press that he happened to have at hand. However, it wasn't until 1909 that he took out a patent on his safety glass, constructed by inserting a sheet of cellulose nitrate between two panes of glass.

His expected market of automobile manufacturers wasn't keen on the innovation, put off by the prospect of high costs. Safety glass got its first 'big break' with the onset of the First World War, when it was used in the lens panels of gas masks. Having thus proved its worth, the motor industry came round to it in the 1920s as the numbers of vehicles and, correspondingly, accidents increased.

A stainless reputation

The invention of stainless steel came about as a result of research into improving British armaments in the early years of the 20th century when the threat of war was growing. The man who created the new alloy had the foresight to see that aside from its massive potential for industrial use, it might also revolutionise domestic life. But before he got to that stage, Harry Brearley had literally thrown his great discovery in the bin.

Brearley was born in 1871 in Sheffield, the traditional centre of the English steel industry. His father worked in it, and at the age of twelve, Harry left school to take a job with him. Having completed evening courses and studies of his own, he was employed as a researcher in the labs of Thomas Firth & Co. Firth joined with another company to form the Brown Firth Research Laboratories and in 1908, amid rising tensions between Europe's great powers, Brearley was asked to head a team to find a way to prevent the interiors of gun barrels from eroding so badly in the high temperatures caused when they were fired.

He started out by experimenting with the addition of varying amounts of carbon and chromium to steel. It was already known that the melting point of steel was raised by adding chromium, and steel and chromium alloys were commonly used in the manufacture of aircraft. The story goes that after experimentation, Brearley would dispose of any unwanted alloy samples into a bin. One day he got rid of a steel–chromium mix he had been working on, which contained about 12 per cent chromium. He thought nothing more about it until he noticed that, despite being exposed to air and water, the metal showed no sign of rusting. Fishing the sample out of the bin, he carried out further tests in which it was exposed to a host of other traditionally corrosive substances. The alloy remain untarnished and, in a moment of minimal originality, Brearley named his new metal 'rustless steel'.

Brearley recognised the vast potential of this new material. He saw how it might be used not just in industrial machinery but in the home too. The company started producing it commercially and, after a suggestion by one of the city's prominent cutlery-makers, it was renamed as 'stainless steel'.

The First World War put a halt on any further developments and Brearley resigned from Brown Firth in 1915 after falling out with his bosses over the issue of patents. However, a new wave of research into stainless steel began in the 1920s under the man who replaced him at the firm, Dr. W.H. Hatfield. In 1924 Hatfield revealed a new stainless steel composition that now also included nickel. It's this mix that remains in common use today.

Its use in the domestic setting was kick-started by an appearance at the 1934 Ideal Home Exhibition in London, where Firth Brown exhibited their 'Staybrite City', filled with cutlery, coffee and tea services, cooking utensils and the like. Brearley died in 1948 and was honoured with a burial in Sheffield Cathedral.

Polytetrafluoroethylene-expialidocious

Another substance widely used in cookware was also discovered by chance. Polytetrafluoroethylene (PTFE), better known by its trademarked name Teflon, was invented in 1938 at DuPont's Jackson Laboratory in New Jersey. A hardwearing and non-reactive plastic, it has proved invaluable in countless environments, from space travel to heart surgery.

Roy J. Plunkett was born in 1910 in Ohio. Having graduated in 1931 from Manchester College, he found his job opportunities limited by the Depression. He decided to carry on with his studies and graduated with a PhD from Ohio State University in 1936, before winning a job as a researcher with the DuPont Company. He was set to work exploring gases that might be used as non-toxic refrigerants.

Among his samples was a tank of a frozen and compressed fluorocarbon, tetrafluoroethylene. On 6 April 1938 Plunkett and his assistant, Jack Rebok, opened the tank, but to their surprise there was no expulsion of gas. They checked the tank's valve to see if something was amiss, but it was fine. Breaking into the tank for a closer look, they discovered that the substance had spontaneously polymerised and formed a waxy white powder.

Further studies on this previously unknown substance

found that it was almost completely inert and incredibly slippery. The lab was soon able to produce this PTFE at will, but they weren't entirely sure of its practical applications. However, the clouds of the Second World War were gathering, and scientists working on the atom bomb found themselves in need of a tough material to use in gaskets that could endure contact with highly reactive gases. The man heading the US Army team in the atom bomb project, General Leslie Groves, had links with DuPont staff and heard talk of the new PTFE. With finances of no concern, PTFE was developed for practical application in the bomb.

As time passed, PTFE was shown to have less sinister uses. Pans and baking tins coated in the non-stick material appeared in the 1960s and it was used as a stain-resistant element in fabrics. But of even greater significance were its medical applications, for instance in pacemakers, artificial joints, dentures and even artificial corneas. It also had a role to play in the space race, being used in the manufacture of space suits and vehicles.

Stocking trade

Nylon is one of the most commonly used synthetic materials in the world, another product of the DuPont laboratories. It was invented in 1934 by the research team of Wallace Carothers, who were partaking in a bit of horseplay while the boss was absent.

Carothers was brought to DuPont from an academic

career at the universities of Illinois and Harvard, where he had a reputation as one of the greatest organic chemists of the age. He was set to work on researching natural polymers like silk and rubber with an eye to producing man-made substitutes. He assembled a team of much-admired scientists but solid progress was slow. When they first created the polyamide, nylon, which had a structure much like that of silk, they observed little potential for it and put it to one side. Instead they worked on polyesters, and it was then that one of the team, Julian Hill, discovered that you could use a glass rod to draw out a ball of polyester and stretch it into silk-like material. This process was known as cold-drawing.

One day when Carothers was on business elsewhere, Hill and his cohorts decided it would be fun to see how far they could stretch the polyesters. The answer was all the way down the corridor. However, the polyesters had limited potential as textiles because of their low melting point, so the team decided to carry out a similar test with the discarded polyamides, including nylon. They found that the cold-drawing significantly strengthened the molecular structure of the nylon. It was apparent that they had a major new discovery on their hands.

DuPont patented the cold-drawing process and nylon was introduced at the 1939 New York World Fair. The first breakout product was nylon stockings, with over four million pairs sold within hours of going on sale in New York in 1940. When the Second World War came, nylon was directed towards more immediate needs like the manufacture of air force parachutes. For women who had been introduced to a wonder product and then had it taken away, the appeal of nylon grew only stronger. Today it's at the heart of a multi-billion-dollar industry. The story for Carothers ended less happily, though. Prone to depression, he became convinced he was spent as a scientific force and committed suicide by poisoning in 1937.

Incidentally, Rayon, another type of artificial silk, had been discovered serendipitously in the 1870s in France by Hilaire de Chardonnet, an assistant to Louis Pasteur. In this period, disease had decimated the country's silkworm population, with serious implications for the silk industry. Pasteur was brought in to investigate a solution and he employed de Chardonnet, who believed that a man-made substitute could be the answer. However, it wasn't until he was working on some photographic plates in a darkroom that he got his unexpected break when he knocked over a bottle of collodion. He didn't bother to clean up the spillage at first and when he eventually got round to it, he found that the chemical had partially evaporated and was now a thick, tacky liquid. When he went to wipe it up, he noticed that it produced long silk-like strands. So began six years of intensive work until he found he could produce the artificial silk from a mixture of mulberry leaves (coincidentally the favoured meal of the silkworm), ether and alcohol, which was then coagulated in a warm air stream. Unveiled at the 1891 Paris Exposition, it was renamed as Rayon in 1924.

The crest of a wave

Percy Spencer was regarded as something of an electronics whizz, particularly for his work that startlingly increased the rate of production of magnetrons. A magnetron is essentially a cathode in a vacuum tube and was key to the radar systems used by the Allied powers during the Second World War. It produces microwaves, which in radar are reflected off a target object via an antenna. These reflected waves are then used to generate a 'radar map'. However, it's doubtful that even he could ever have dreamed that his radar work would eventually lead to the invention of the microwave oven, one of the vital ingredients for a successful life as a modern couch potato.

Spencer was born in Howland, Maine, in 1897. His father died when he was two and his mother turned Percy over to the care of an aunt and uncle. Leaving school at just twelve years of age, he got a job working in a mill. Shortly after beginning work there, the mill was electrified, a technological development that captured Spencer's imagination. He later served in the navy, where he picked up knowledge of wireless telegraphy. When he was in his twenties, he managed to get a job with the Raytheon Company and over the subsequent years built a reputation as a truly brilliant researcher and technician, particularly in the field of radar technology. He accumulated 300 separate patents during his lifetime.

Given the Distinguished Public Service Award by the US Navy for his work on developing easier-to-build and cheaper magnetrons, Spencer continued his research after the Second

World War ended. It was in late 1945 that he endured the somewhat disconcerting sensation of a peanut chocolate bar melting in his trouser pocket as he conducted his work around a magnetron. However, he was able to rise above his inevitable feelings of dismay and set his mind to explaining just what had happened. He soon realised that the answer must lie with the microwaves being emitted by the magnetron. Waves strong enough to cook food.

Keen to test out his thesis, he ordered up some popcorn kernels and set them down beside the machine. Sure enough, he soon had corn popping around his lab. The following day he tried cooking an egg which, we're led to believe, exploded in the face of a colleague. Spencer carried on developing a workable prototype and was ready to sell his first microwave within two years – essentially a metal box that channelled the microwaves towards the food put inside it. It was truly a beast, standing over 5½ feet tall and weighing in at three quarters of a ton. This first generation of machines sold almost exclusively to commercial caterers, although many chefs reportedly grew frustrated at its inability to brown or crisp-up food.

It took several more decades of development before it became feasible to have microwaves in the average home. By 1970, the year that Spencer died, sales were stuck around the 40,000 mark. Within five years, a million were being sold annually, and current estimates reckon 90 per cent of all American homes now have one. Impressive statistics for a machine that might never have been invented had Percy's sweet tooth not caused him to smuggle a snack into his lab.

Strike a light!

The first friction matches were invented by an English chemist in the second quarter of the 19th century. Their creation was the result of John Walker's fascination with firearms and their associated combustible powders. While he had the sagacity to develop his discovery into a saleable product, alas for him he didn't quite have the foresight to realise that it could make his fortune. That honour fell to an entrepreneurial Londoner called Samuel Johnson, who took the devilishly good invention and marketed them as 'Lucifers'.

John Walker was born in 1781 in Stockton-on-Tees. The son of a grocer and wine merchant, he was put through grammar school, leaving at fifteen years of age to take up an apprenticeship with a local surgeon, Watson Alcock. Walker then went to London to continue his academic studies, before returning to Stockton as Alcock's assistant. He also went to York and Durham to train alongside wholesale drug-gists. In 1819 Walker opened his own pharmacy on the town's high street. Dressed in trademark tall beaver hat, white cravat, stockings, breeches and tail-coat, he was a well-known figure around the town.

He retained a keen interest in chemistry in its broadest forms and had a nice sideline providing the local gunsmith with an assortment of suitable powders and chemicals. In 1826 he was working with a mixture of potassium chlorate, antimony sulphide and gum, which he stirred with a wooden stick. The mixture congealed around the stick and when he accidentally struck it against his kitchen hearth, he saw how it caught light. Walker set to work on creating useable matches with this special formula and, despite their slight unpredictability and imposing smell, he made his first commercial sale (to a local solicitor) in April 1827.

Walker sold his 'Friction Lights' as 'Congreves', a reference to the Congreve Rocket, a weapon then in use with the British Army. The price was a shilling for 100, and tuppence if you wanted a tin, but sales were slow and Walker made little money. He also neglected to patent his idea and in 1830 Samuel Johnson did so instead, selling his 'Lucifers' with almost immediate success. Walker continued to dedicate himself to his various scientific researches until his death in 1859.

A purple patch

The synthetic dye industry began to grow only in the second half of the 19th century when an overly-ambitious chemistry undergraduate failed in his bid to rid the world of malaria but succeeded instead in manufacturing the first synthetic dye, mauve. In the years since, the business has had more than its fair share of serendipitous discoveries.

In 1856 the eighteen-year-old William Perkin was on his holidays from the Royal College of Chemistry. He had decided to try to synthesise quinine, the cure for malaria derived from a rare type of tree (see page 99). The project was, frankly, beyond Perkin and indeed it would be almost another hundred years before anyone mastered its synthesis.

He used aniline as his base material, a by-product of coal tar which itself was waste material produced by the steel industry. By the addition of carbon and hydrogen he created something that was a dark sludge and definitely wasn't quinine. However, when he used alcohol to clean his apparatus, he noticed that the black substance created a deep purple solution. Further tests showed that this solution would stain both silk and cotton a brilliant purple colour. Purple was traditionally one of the most expensive of all natural dyes (requiring the harvesting of huge numbers of special molluscs), hence the association of royalty with the colour. Perkin saw he was on to a potential winner. He persuaded his father to finance the building of a factory, secured a patent, worked hard on an economic method of industrial production and made himself a personal fortune.

Then in 1893 a chemist by the name of Sapper, working in the labs of the German company BASF, cack-handedly discovered a way to synthesise indigo, a dye previously obtainable only from cultivated plants. Again, coal-tar provided the base material: naphthalene. Sapper was boiling this up with sulphuric acid when he managed to break a thermometer, sending a dose of mercury into the mix. This addition precipitated a series of reactions that converted the naphthalene into phthalic anhydride. From this indigo could be extracted with relative ease, a process perfected by BASF's Karl Heumann. When synthetic indigo came on the market in 1897, it quickly sidelined demand for the natural variant.

Monastral blue, a deep, rich, vibrant pigment – pigments

being, in contrast to dyes, insoluble in water – was the work of A.G. Dandridge, a chemist with Scottish Dyes Ltd. In 1928 he was overseeing a process by which a compound, phthalimide, was produced by combining ammonia with molten phthalic anhydride in a large iron vat. One particular day he noticed that unusual blue crystals had formed on the iron. The metal used in the manufacture of the vat was combining with its contents to create a new pigment. Further tests revealed that different blue and green pigments were created in the presence of nickel and copper, rather than iron. It was copper that produced monastral blue. This group of phthalocyanine pigments has subsequently found widespread use among artists, printers and industrialists.

Under wraps

Jacques E. Brandenberger, a Swiss chemist, came up with the idea of a wipe-clean tablecloth. While his attempts in that direction failed, he did create cellophane, a thin, clear film with a multitude of industrial uses but best known as a material for wrapping food to keep it fresh.

Brandenberger was born in Zurich in 1872. He studied chemistry and began life as a textile engineer. At the turn of the century he was dining out one evening when he spotted a fellow diner knock over a glass of wine across a tablecloth. There was something of a kerfuffle as the waiter set about replacing the cloth with a clean one, and it occurred to Brandenberger how much easier it would have been to simply give it a quick wipe-down.

He thus set his mind to inventing a suitable coating that could be used to make fabrics waterproof and protect them from stains. He tried out various possible chemicals including, in 1908, liquid viscose which he derived from wood cellulose. He hung up a cloth and gave it a thorough spray with the liquid. Unfortunately, as it dried, the cloth became stiff and impractical to use. However, he noted that the viscose coating could be peeled off the fabric as a thin sheet of transparent film. His thoughts now turned to how he might make use of it.

He soon developed a machine that could manufacture the cellophane sheets and set about patenting the material and its associated technology. By 1912 he was marketing the product for use in gas masks. In 1923 he sold the rights to manufacture and sell it in North America to the DuPont Cellophane Company (continuing DuPont's long tradition of accepting the gifts of serendipity). A DuPont research team led by William Hale Charch managed to find a way to waterproof cellophane by 1927, opening up the crucial food packaging market. In the decade to 1938, US sales of cellophane tripled; and in 1938 it was responsible for 25 per cent of DuPont's profits.

All sewn up

Elias Howe was a pioneer of the sewing machine, eventually making a fortune from his invention. Most early types of sewing machine were either inefficient or impracticably

177

expensive. Howe spent many years developing a rival machine that was both labour-saving and economic. A key element of his machine came not from endless hours of toil in his workshop but from a dream he had about being captured by cannibals.

Howe was born on 9 July 1819 in Spencer, Massachusetts. As a teenager he was apprenticed in a textile factory but within two years an economic downturn saw him unemployed. He then moved to Boston where he found work with Ari Davis, an instrument-maker. By the late 1830s a number of prototype sewing machines had already been introduced by the likes of Barthélemy Thimonnier in France and Walter Hunt in the USA, but none were 'the finished product'. Ari imbued Howe with the notion that the man who could perfect the sewing machine would make himself a fortune.

When still in his twenties, Howe succumbed to serious ill health and had to give up work. His wife took up sewing as a means of supporting their young family. Howe realised that the trick would be to devise a machine that didn't try to replicate a human's actions but which had a technology all of its own.

Then one night in 1845 Howe had his strange dream. He dreamt he was being pursued by cannibals and was eventually caught and deposited in a boiling cauldron. All his attempts to extricate himself from the pot were snuffed out by guards poking him back in with their spears. When he woke up from this nightmare, his first recollections seemed to offer few practical solutions to the sewing machine conundrum. But then he remembered a minor detail about the guards. They each held a spear with a hole in it, near the sharpened head. This proved to be Howe's intellectual breakthrough.

He immediately began work on a machine with a needle where the eye was close to the tip, rather than at the other end as was usual. This allowed for a process whereby the needle pushed through a piece of fabric, creating a loop of thread on the opposite side. A shuttle then slipped thread from a second source through the loop, creating a highly effective tight lock stitch. Howe patented his system in 1846.

Howe's path to riches didn't open up immediately. He had to overcome setbacks including his workshop burning down, long patent disputes, dishonest agents and a lack of entrepreneurial drive. After an unsuccessful foray into Europe, he returned to the USA to find that Isaac Singer had rather stolen his thunder with his own much-loved machine. However, Singer was eventually ordered to pay some $15,000 to his rival in back royalties. In 1856 an agreement was reached between several sewing machine manufacturers that saw them pool their patents. Under the terms of the agreement, Howe received $5 for each machine sold in the States and $1 for those elsewhere. The deal earned him some $2 million. But he didn't have long to enjoy his money. He died in 1867 at the age of 48, his life's struggles finally catching up with him.

Pie in the sky

The Frisbee was one of the great leisure items of the last century and owed its popularity not to some highly planned marketing campaign by a toy manufacturer but to the ingenuity of some students with a penchant for pre-made pies.

The game of friends throwing a light disc to each other first found popularity in the grounds of the University of Yale in Connecticut. However, the discs were not of the type with which we are now familiar. In fact, they were tins used since the 1870s by the Frisbie Bakery in Bridgeport, Connecticut to supply their pies. The original 'Frisbie' turned out to be a snack and a toy rolled into one!

Walter F. Morrison (and his then business partner, Warren Franscioni) developed the first modern plastic 'Frisbie' in 1948. However, it didn't really take off (in terms of sales at least) until Morrison struck out alone and marketed his creation as a Pluto Platter. The owners of the Wham-O Manufacturing Company cottoned on to its mass appeal in the mid-1950s and bought the rights from Morrison. They renamed the Platter as the Frisbee (a nod to its early history) and sold over 100 million units before selling on the patent to toy giants Mattel. Morrison himself became a millionaire from the royalties.

Another toy created by chance was the Slinky, the metal coil that seemed to 'walk' down stairs of its own volition, to the delight of countless children and adults. It was the creation of Richard James in 1943. James, a naval engineer, was researching tension springs for use on board ships.

When one fell from a shelf in his lab, he was intrigued by the way it made its way end-over-end down to the floor. He managed to persuade his initially sceptical wife, Betty, that this could be a new toy. They took out a bank loan to manu-facture 400 Slinkys (a name chosen by Betty from the Swedish word for sleek and sinuous) and debuted them at a store called Gimbels in Philadelphia. The entire stock, priced at a dollar each, sold out in an hour and a half.

Sales have never really slowed, with the Slinky notching up over 300 million sales around the world. Nonetheless, Richard James grew tired of his creation and left his family in 1960 to follow a religious calling in Bolivia. Betty continued to run the company they had set up until her death in 2008. She was always determined that the Slinky would remain affordable for everyone and, at the time of her death, the price was still only $5 apiece.

CHAPTER 12

Treasure Trove

Every weekend, beaches and fields throughout the land are populated by individuals belonging to the genus *amateur metal detector*, convinced that one day they will stumble upon unimaginable riches. Far more romantic, though, are those discoveries made by pure serendipity. In his 1991 novel, *The Last Voyage of Somebody the Sailor*, John Barth told the story of a journalist lost overboard off the coast of Serendib (a variant spelling of Serendip, the old Persian name for Sri Lanka). He wrote: '[Y]ou don't reach Serendib by plotting a course for it. You have to set out in good faith for elsewhere and lose your bearings ... serendipitously.'

The hen-pecked doctor

Many of us in a moment of vanity may have dreamed of being immortalised in a great work of art. The opportunity falls to very few, though. For Dr Felix Rey, a young doctor working at a hospital at Arles in France in the late 19th century, the chance came out of the blue when Vincent Van Gogh became his patient. Yet the portrait that the great master produced was treated so abysmally that perhaps Rey's greatest stroke of fortune came in rescuing it twenty years after he had given it away.

Van Gogh, perhaps the greatest of the post-Impressionists, was a latecomer to painting. Born in the Netherlands in 1853, it wasn't until 1880 that he began to paint in earnest. Prone to dark depressions, he travelled extensively and in 1888 arrived in Arles, where he worked with another great artist, Paul Gauguin, whom he had befriended in Paris the previous year.

Towards the end of 1888 the friendship was falling apart and Van Gogh was succumbing to his demons. On a fateful day in December of that year he pursued Gauguin with a razor before returning to his home and slicing off a piece of his own ear, which he then presented to a local prostitute. He was arrested and put into the care of the local hospital, lapsing into an acute psychotic state and spending three days in solitary confinement.

Rey was put in charge of Van Gogh's care and was the first doctor to diagnose his epilepsy. Prescribing him potassium bromide, he oversaw the artist's return to relative stability and Van Gogh was allowed back home after a few weeks. However, the hallucinations and psychotic episodes soon returned (and were probably not ameliorated by his taste for absinthe). Thirty of Vincent's neighbours signed a petition for him to be removed from the town.

Rey continued to show his patient great care and kindness, and Van Gogh decided to paint a portrait of him as a gift in recognition. When Rey was presented with the finished work, notable for Van Gogh's idiosyncratic use of colour, he described being 'horrified' at the sight. What was he to make of this vision with red hair ('I really did not have red hair'), outlined in green? Deciding against giving it pride of place on his own wall, he gave it to his parents who were equally appalled. However, his mother, being practical of mind, did find a purpose for it. She used it to block up a hole in one of the family chicken coops.

Van Gogh famously sold only one painting during his lifetime. Yet his death prompted a reappraisal of his output (some 900 paintings) and his genius was ultimately recognised. In such a climate, it was hardly surprising that Rey might have reconsidered his own hasty actions. Two decades after giving away the painting, he returned to claim it back. Remarkably, it had survived unscathed during its long years at the mercy of pecking beaks and the unpredictable elements. It now resides at the Pushkin State Museum of Fine Arts in Moscow as a key work by one of art's most influential exponents. Just what the doctor ordered.

Saints alive!

Fra Angelico (born as Guido di Pietro in Tuscany at the end of the 14th century) was one of the great artists of Renaissance Italy. Already a renowned painter before he took holy orders, his biographer, Vasari, called him a 'rare and perfect talent'. Among his most important commissions was a series of eight panels for an altarpiece for the convent of San Marco in Florence. The work was split up at some point during the Napoleonic wars and, though six of the panels were recovered, two seemed lost forever. Then in 2007 the family of a recently deceased academic from Oxford rediscovered the lost masterpieces hanging on the door of her spare room.

Painted in 1439, each of the eight panels celebrated a separate saint. The whereabouts of the missing two panels had been one of the art world's enduring mysteries. It turned out that Jean Preston, an expert in medieval handwriting who lived a very modest lifestyle, had stumbled across the paintings in California in the 1960s. She had no idea of their provenance but liked the look of them. Paying no more than £200, she gave them as a present to her art-loving father. When he died in 1974, they came down to her.

She then hung them in the spare room of her two-up/two-down home in Oxford, where they remained for the next 33 years. When she died in 2007, aged 77, her family called in a local auctioneers to value her estate. They knew the pictures were good, but it fell to an old family friend, Michael Liversidge, formerly head of Bristol University's History of Art department, to identify them. The pictures, tempera paint on poplar wood with a gold leaf background, measured just 15in x 5in (38cm x 13cm) and had been commissioned by the legendary patron of the arts and ruler of Florence, Cosimo de Medici.

The panels were auctioned at Duke's Saleroom in Dorset

in 2007 and were sold to a private buyer for £1.7 million. One of the saints depicted was positively identified as St Vincent Ferrer, the patron saint of builders and, perhaps, of medieval handwriting experts too.

Fish wife

Jan Van Eyck was born in 1395 in the Bishopric of Liège in what is now Belgium but was then the Holy Roman Empire. As one of the most important artists of the Northern Renaissance, he became inextricably linked with Bruges, where he died in 1441. Among his most admired works is an intimate portrait of his wife, Margareta. Now one of the most popular exhibits in the city's Groeninge Museum, for a while it looked destined for a rather more humble existence until its fortuitous rediscovery.

The half-length oil portrait of Margareta catches her in a three-quarter pose, attired in a scarlet gown and white hood. It shows her as a real woman, intelligent and strong but not a classical beauty. There are two inscriptions on the painting. The first translates as: 'My husband Johannes finished painting me on 15 June in the year 1439, when I was 33.' The other is van Eyck's motto, 'To the best of my ability', rendered in Greek lettering.

The painting had belonged to the Bruges Guild of Painters and Saddlers, in whose chapel it was shown every Saint Luke's Day, as if it were a holy relic. The rest of the time it was safely locked away. In 1794 the country fell under the rule of the French First Republic, which plundered many great works of art and took them to Paris. The painting of Margareta avoided this unwanted move because of a complex mortgage that the Guild had on its property. Nonetheless, at some point shortly afterwards the picture went missing.

Then in 1808 Peter Van Lede was walking through the city's Vismarkt, or fish market, which specialised in selling the finest produce fresh from the North Sea. As he inspected a particularly enticing display, he noticed something vaguely suspicious about the tray on which the fish had been placed. A closer look confirmed it to be Van Eyck's lost masterpiece. Van Lede, being admirably public-spirited, rescued the painting and made a gift of it to the city.

Undercover detective

It's a very British pleasure to trawl the shelves of your high street Oxfam shop, rifling through the volumes of Jeffrey Archer and Jackie Collins or old *Reader's Digests* in the hope of uncovering a gem. More usually, the customer will return home to content themselves with a Jilly Cooper omnibus and an old Rick Astley cassette. However, two volunteers at the Harrogate branch of Oxfam did indeed stumble upon a literary diamond as they sorted through the latest lot of donations.

Ken Lowe, a retired maths teacher, and Rosie Beer, a retired medical practitioner, volunteered at the shop, helping with internet sales and researching any items that looked like they might be a little out of the ordinary. In 2003 they began looking through a box of anonymous donations when their collective eye was caught by a bound edition of various Victorian *Beeton's Christmas Annuals*. They put the volume to one side for further investigation, but the shop was just about to undergo a series of major overhauls and it was a full three years before they got round to some serious detective work.

A close inspection revealed that the collection included the Annual for 1887. Among the stories it contained was one by Arthur Conan Doyle called *A Study in Scarlet*. This just so happened to be the first appearance of Sherlock Holmes, a veritable holy grail for aficionados of detective fiction the world over. Including the Harrogate edition, only 31 copies of the original story were known to be in existence, with only about a third of those in the possession of private owners.

The two volunteers were something of a crack team when it came to unearthing treasures, having previously turned up a first edition of J. R. R. Tolkien's *The Return of the King* (the third instalment of the *Lord of the Rings* trilogy) as well as a valuable report from the 1908 Olympic Games. However, these paled against this Holmes find. The auctioneers Bonham's held a sale in Oxford in May 2008, at which around 100 rare books were sold on behalf of Oxfam. *A Study in Scarlet* was the star, the hammer finally falling at £15,500.

An Oxfam shop in Bangor, Wales, was the beneficiary of another extraordinary donation in 2007. Marilyn Willis was the keen-eyed volunteer on that occasion, spotting that a first edition of *Le Ballet* by Boris Kochno included a valuable lithograph by Pablo Picasso, perhaps the most famous artist of the 20th century.

The following year, a charity shop across the Atlantic in Maryland received a fetching painting of a Parisian street scene. It was all set to be tagged at $20, a usual price for the large numbers of chocolate box-type pictures the shop received. However, once again, an eagle-eyed employee suspected that there was something special about this item. Calling in the experts, it was identified as 'Marché aux fleurs', painted early in the 20th century by the French Impressionist, Edouard-Léon Cortès. It was subsequently sold by Sotheby's for over $40,000.

Bargain buys

For the aspirational bargain hunter, thankfully not every shop has a Ken Lowe, Rosie Beer or Marilyn Willis. Now and again it's the customer who comes out on top.

In 1989 a financial analyst was wandering around an antiques market in Adamstown, Pennsylvania. He took a fancy to a frame holding a decrepit and fairly nondescript pastoral scene, and so negotiated a sale with the stall-owner. He paid the princely sum of $4.

When he got back home, the buyer set about disassociating the frame from the picture, but as he set to work he was rather disgruntled to find the frame falling apart in his hands. Then he noticed a folded sheet of paper resting between the canvas and the frame's wooden panel. Intrigued, he unfolded the paper and discovered a copy of the US Declaration of Independence.

Wary that it might simply be a cheap reproduction, he had the document checked out by experts in Philadelphia. They confirmed that it was one of 500 official copies made from the original Declaration in 1776. Of those 500, only 24 were known to have survived, and only three of those were in private hands. In 1991 it was auctioned by Sotheby's, selling for a considerably more princely $2,400,000.

Some fifteen years later, another copy of the Declaration, this one commissioned in 1820 by John Quincy Adams (America's president from 1825–29), turned up in a second-hand shop in Nashville, Tennessee. It was sold by the unsuspecting proprietor to one Michael Sparks for $2.50. It was auctioned the following year for just shy of $500,000.

In 2008 back in Britain, Mark Lawrence, a keen young art enthusiast, was rather taken with a small painting on copper that he saw in the window of an antique shop in Windsor. According to an accreditation on its frame, it was the work of the Italian Renaissance artist, Palma Vecchio, although it seemed more likely it was a Victorian copy. Lawrence decided to splash out £350 on the piece and then engaged the services of a restorer friend to give it a clean.

Keen to know more about his purchase, Lawrence took the painting to the nearby Museum of Reading. The curator there believed it did indeed date to the right period for

Vecchio, who was Venice's principal artist at the end of the 16th century. The National Gallery in London was contacted to undertake further study on the painting, but they concluded that it had indeed been mis-attributed. It was actually a lost work, *St Jerome In the Wilderness*, by Vecchio's nephew, Palma Giovane, and dated to around 1595. Its estimated value was £250,000.

Dadd's Sunday best

The Antiques Roadshow is a staple of British Sunday evenings, a chance to peek at the nation's hidden treasures, to share the joy when an heirloom turns out to be priceless or, equally, to wallow in the schadenfreude as that beautiful gem-encrusted Fabergé egg turns out to have been made three years ago from fool's gold and coloured glass. But in 1987 one couple got to live the dream when they ambled into an episode of the *Roadshow* to learn that they owned a lost masterpiece.

On that particular day, filming was taking place at a hall in Barnstaple in Devon and there had been relatively few notable items going past the show's panel of experts. It was mid-afternoon when a local married couple who had recently retired decided to take their dog for a walk. They followed the hound's choice of route, which involved going through a park that backed on to the hall where the Roadshow was being held. They decided they might as well make the most of this opportunity to learn more about a watercolour that had hung on their wall for many years, despite it not being a particular favourite. It had been a gift to them from someone or other's mother-in-law.

They were sent in the direction of one of the show's experts, Peter Nahum, who suspected from the outset that here was something rather exciting. He wanted time to double-check his suspicions, but he strongly suspected that he was looking at *The Halt in the Desert*, a painting by the Victorian master Richard Dadd that had fallen off the radar for some 130 years.

Richard Dadd had been born in 1817 and was considered a highly promising young artist when, in 1842, he went on a tour of Europe and the Middle East with his patron, Sir Thomas Phillips. What occurred on this trip isn't clear, but when Dadd returned home the following year, his mental state was ravaged. He stabbed his father to death before being certified insane, living out his remaining 42 years in asylums. It was in the early days of his institutionalisation that he painted *The Halt in the Desert*, which went missing some time around 1857.

Nahum broke with *Roadshow* tradition and declined to value the work on the spot. Instead he asked permission to have it authenticated after the show and it was independently valued at £100,000. The British Museum was keen to secure this long-lost national treasure and was an eager buyer, significantly boosting the pension fund of Barnstaple's luckiest dog-walkers.

One man's art, another man's rubbish

In 2003 Elizabeth Gibson was buying a coffee in Manhattan's Upper West Side when she spotted a painted canvas in among someone's rubbish. Succumbing to the magpie within her, she decided to rescue it and take it back to her flat. Over the next few years she did some research into the work, discovering that she had liberated a million-dollar painting and solved a twenty-year-old crime into the bargain.

Gibson was following her customary practice of getting a morning caffeine fix when she spotted the picture, which measured about four feet by three. Her eye was caught by its bright colours and she extricated it with only about twenty minutes to go before the garbage truck was due on its rounds. Back at home she hung it on her wall, noting a signature, 'Tamayo 0-70'.

Over time she decided to try to learn more about her find. A friend told her that Rufino Tamayo was a much-respected Mexican Modernist who could command high prices. However, it was only when Gibson went to the library and found a book about him with her painting on the cover that she began to realise she might have something very special. If the pictures were indeed the same, she was in possession of *Tres Personajes*, regarded as an abstract masterpiece from the artist's later years.

Some more delving turned up an old episode of the American version of *The Antiques Roadshow*, which featured a strand on missing artworks. *Tres Personajes*, it turned out, had been stolen from a couple in the late 1980s during a house move. The husband had bought it for his wife in 1977 for $50,000. A $15,000 reward for its safe recovery remained uncollected.

Gibson arranged to meet August Uribe, one of the experts on *The Antiques Roadshow*, and he confirmed that the picture was all that it purported to be. So arrangements got under way for its return to its rightful owners, who decided to put it up for auction. Sotheby's sold it in late 2007 for a price of $1,049,000. Gibson for her part picked up the $15,000 reward as well as a finder's fee from the auction house.

School fate

Many children make an art form out of avoiding the school library, but one keen ten-year-old became so fascinated by a painting that hung over his school librarian's desk that he embarked on an academic quest to find out more about it. It proved a most worthwhile use of his time.

It was 2000 when Bingham Bryant, a pupil at Old Lyme Center School in Connecticut, first spotted the rather grimy old depiction of Persephone being abducted by Pluto, god of the underworld. Young Bingham's father, Christopher, was a dealer in military antiques. Son persuaded father that they should embark on a research project to find out about the captivating picture.

After a lot of detective work and scouring through art books, the team discovered that this was *The Fate of*

Persephone by the acclaimed British artist, Walter Crane. Crane was an artist and illustrator born in Liverpool in 1845 and was particularly associated with the Arts and Crafts movement. He painted *The Fate of Persephone* in 1878 and it was exhibited at the Grosvenor Gallery summer exhibition that year. It came into German hands early the next century but record of it ended in 1923.

The Bryants subsequently learned that it later found its way to a Yale professor, Bryan Hooker, who loaned it to his cousin who was then working in Old Lyme. It had hung in the school library, unframed, since 1935, all memory of its wonderful provenance lost. At least until Bingham entered the scene.

The painting was auctioned by Christie's in London and made $560,000, which went to Hooker's heirs. Bingham received a finder's fee and started a new life at an English boarding school, where he promised to keep his eye out for any other lost treasures.

A fishy disappearance

Hermann Sudermann was born in Prussia in 1857 and made his name as a novelist and playwright of the naturalistic school. He didn't come from a wealthy background, and in the early days of his career he financed himself by writing fiction which was published in newspapers in instalments. To begin with he would be paid chapter by chapter, but his editor grew concerned about what would happen if

Sudermann were unable to finish a story. The newspaper's readership wouldn't accept a story only half-told. Therefore, a new arrangement was agreed that publication wouldn't begin until the whole novel was in the bag.

In 1887 he set to work on *Frau Sorge*, which was to tell of the experiences of a young man whose loyalties were split between his father and the woman he loved. As soon as Sudermann had finished it, he was keen to get it into the hands of his editor so that he might replenish his depleted coffers. With the manuscript tucked into his coat pocket, Sudermann set out for Berlin via Insterburg, where he was to meet some friends.

Alas, Sudermann's good intentions to catch the first available connection to Berlin fell by the wayside as he enjoyed the company of his chums. When he awoke the following day he did find himself in Berlin, but he had no idea how he came to be there and realised to his horror that he was *sans Frau Sorge*.

Utterly crestfallen and cursing his own foolishness, Sudermann headed back home with his tail firmly between his legs. Some 24 hours after his night of ill-advised revelry, the author found himself back in Insterberg. To add insult to injury, there was no connecting train until the following morning, so he was forced to shell out for a room. He then set out around the town's public houses in a bid to drown his well-founded sorrows.

Afflicted by a bout of alcohol-induced munchies, he stopped off at a delicatessen and purchased himself a herring.

The proprietor wrapped it neatly for his customer in some paper taken from a bundle close to him. As he handed the package to Sudermann, the writer noticed something eerily familiar about the handwriting on the paper. It was his own. Promptly unpacking the fish, he saw that here was a page of his lost manuscript. The delicatessen owner handed over his newly-acquired pile of scrap paper, which was virtually the complete book. Another trip to Berlin beckoned and *Frau Sorge* was published later in 1887 to major commercial and critical acclaim.

Fishmongers and the manuscripts of great writers continued to have a strange affinity. In 1995 a previously unknown letter by Dylan Thomas to his future wife, Caitlin Macnamara, was put up for auction by Ruth Cutler, the daughter of a fishmonger called Thomas Topp. The fishmonger had come into possession of it several decades earlier when it was given to him, either by Caitlin herself or a member of her family, for the purpose of wrapping fish ready for delivery. Fortunately, Mrs Topp had been so overwhelmed by the poetical beauty of the letter ('I love you for millions and millions of things, clocks and vampires and dirty nails and squiggly paintings and lovely hair and being dizzy and falling dreams') that she rescued it. It achieved an auction price of just under £4,000.

CHAPTER 13

A Final Miscellany

This last selection includes examples of serendipity that just didn't fit in anywhere else. All of which goes to prove that there are no hard-and-fast rules about when or where good fortune will strike, or for whom.

Leaning tower of Pisa

When Pisa decided to construct a bell tower in the 12th century, it was an expression of the town's success – a prestige construction to match those of its rivals, including Florence and Genoa. Today, Pisa owes its worldwide fame to the tower and its distinctive lean, the unexpected result of some medieval cowboy builders laying shoddy foundations.

Pisa is situated on the Arno river in Tuscany and came to prominence as one of the region's great maritime republics. Work began in 1173 on what was to be a 180-foot-high campanile (bell tower) in white marble. Incredibly, its foundations were dug to a depth of only 10 feet into what proved to be unstable soil. The tower's lean, to the south-west, was obvious to the naked eye as early as completion of the first three storeys in 1178.

There was then a pause in construction as the town's fortunes took a downturn. Pisa was engaged in almost incessant conflict with Florence, Genoa and Lucca over the next hundred years, and building began again only in 1272. The warring did bring one benefit, though – the soil on which the tower stood was given time to settle, preventing the lean from getting perilously worse. The new builders sought to compensate for the structural frailties by building the subsequent floors with one side higher than the other. In this way the lean was turned into a slight curve.

Military defeat to Genoa in 1284 halted work once more. It wasn't until 1319 that the seventh floor was in place, and it would be over 50 years more before the bell chamber (the tower's *raison d'être*, after all) was completed. As it stands today in the Piazza del Duomo – alongside Pisa's cathedral, baptistry and cemetery – the tower measures 183ft 3in (55.9 metres) and numbers eight storeys, reached by 296 steps. Its angle of slant is 3.97° or 12ft 10in (3.9 m) from the vertical.

In the mid-1960s an international team of engineers sought to stabilise the tower to prevent its collapse, but without reversing the trademark tilt. In 1990, when the lean had reached 14ft 6in, the tower was closed to the public for eleven years for repairs. A large amount of soil was removed from around the base, straightening the tower by 18 inches. Its tilt thus replicated that which existed as of 1838. By 2008 further earthworks had ensured the tower's stability for at least the next two centuries.

The identity of the tower's architect remains a mystery and

is the subject of heated debate. One wonders whether the man responsible would bathe in the glory of designing one of the world's most recognisable buildings or cringe at its evident structural inadequacies. Had the original design and build gone a little more smoothly, Pisa might well have declined into a small town lost among the footnotes of history.

A case of identity

Everyone knows what Sherlock Holmes, the most famous fictional detective in the world, looks like: the tall, striking figure adorned with a deerstalker hat and Inverness cape that has so conquered the popular imagination. Yet this image came not from the pen of Holmes's author, Conan Doyle, but from the man who illustrated so many of the stories for *The Strand* magazine, Sidney Paget. If that were not irony enough, *The Strand* had never meant to employ Sidney at all but wanted his brother, Walter, instead.

The editors of the newly-established *Strand* believed their key to success was to have an illustration on every page. They initially signed up Conan Doyle to write a series of twelve short stories featuring his recurring hero, Sherlock Holmes, to be published monthly in 1891 and 1892. When they were deciding who should draw the accompanying pictures, their minds turned to Walter Paget.

Walter was Sidney's elder brother and by far the more famous, having won particular praise for his illustrations of Daniel Defoe's *Robinson Crusoe*. Sidney, on the other hand, was still trying to win a name for himself, often tackling war subjects such as the conflicts in Egypt and Sudan. However, *The Strand*'s editors didn't have the right contact information for Walter and somehow the commission they had intended for him ended up in the hands of Sidney. One theory goes that they sent the commission to the brothers' father and it was he who passed it on to the wrong son.

It proved to be a huge stroke of good fortune for all involved (with the possible exception of Walter). Sidney was soon producing his iconic drawings and Sherlock became a household name. Walter still managed to make a contribution too, for there's strong evidence that Sidney used him as the model for Holmes.

Conan Doyle wasn't always a Paget fan because he felt that Sidney had made Holmes rather better-looking than the author had intended. However, it would seem that he was eventually won over, for he especially requested Sidney to illustrate *The Hound of the Baskervilles*. As *The Strand* itself put it, Sidney's 'delineations of the famous "Sherlock Holmes" stories had their share in the popularity of that wonderful detective'.

Putting your foot in it

Cinderella is perhaps the greatest fairytale of them all, a rags-to-riches tale incorporating a battle between good and evil with a generous dose of romance thrown in. And there, glistening at its centre, is the iconic image of the glass slipper that will fit only the foot of the fair maiden who has stolen the heart of Prince Charming. It's an extraordinary image, unprecedented anywhere else in literature. To this day there's much debate as to how the 'glass slipper' came into being, and there's a strong argument that it was the result of a fortuitous bit of mistranslation. Was Cinderella's footwear originally made from simple, run-of-the-mill fur?

The exact origins of the Cinderella story aren't clear, but there are comparable tales to be found in the cultures of ancient Greece, Egypt and China (the latter including a reference to a golden slipper). The narrative with which we are familiar today can be traced back to a French version of the story written at the end of the 17th century by Charles Perrault. It was this take on the legend that introduced such notable features as the pumpkin coach, the fairy godmother and, indeed, the glass slippers.

So where did such a wonderfully original idea as the glass slippers come from? Should we simply credit the genius of Perrault? Or do we owe it to a mix-up between the phrases 'pantoufle de vair' ('fur slipper') and 'pantoufle de verre' ('glass slipper')? It was long held that the misinterpretation occurred when an English translator mistook Perrault's 'vair' for 'verre'. It was subsequently shown that Perrault used 'verre' in his original manuscript so that explanation was eventually undermined. However, some critics now argue that it was Perrault who made the mistranslation, perhaps misunderstanding the use of the old-fashioned 'vair' in an oral rendition of the story.

What remains is an enduring symbol of the victory of romantic love. It may be doing Perrault a disservice to suggest that it wasn't the fruit of his rich imagination. Yet to think that it might have been the product of an honest mistake surely only adds to its aura of romanticism.

A yen for gambling

In December 2005 Tetsuya Ichimura, a young stock market speculator, made a personal fortune when a trader at Japanese brokerage firm, Mizuho Securities, made a slip-up on his computer keyboard.

Ichimura was keeping an eye on the stocks of a recruitment company called J-Com and decided to stump up 2·81 billion yen (£13·7 million) for 3,701 shares. He was then somewhat surprised when he saw an offer emanating from Mizuho – 610,000 shares for just one yen (about a cent) each. The Mizuho trader had managed to reverse his figures, having meant to offer one share for 610,000 yen.

The offer prompted an inevitable collapse in J-Com's share price and trading in the company was suspended. To rectify the calamity, the Tokyo Stock Exchange clearing house imposed a settlement on Mizuho and, under its terms, Ichimura traded them his shares for 3·38 billion yen (£16·5 million). With a profit of 0·57 billion yen (£2·8 million), it was a tidy few days' work by any standard.

Ichimura wasn't alone in profiting from this devastating piece of mistyping. Several institutional investors also made a fortune, with Swiss investment bank UBS making upwards of £50 million. Along with several other major investors, they agreed to put the proceeds of their good fortune into a fund to be used for worthy causes. Mizuho, on the other hand, had to weather the loss of over 40 billion yen (over £200 million). One wonders if the flawed trader managed to compose a resignation letter free of any more typos.

A date with destiny

H. L. Mencken was one of the great American critics, a lifelong newspaper man who loved to provoke reaction. A national institution, he was famously a bachelor who didn't really seem to believe in the workability of the institution of marriage. At least, not until he met the woman he would ultimately wed, Sara Haart. Their love affair began at a lecture Mencken was giving at Goucher College, Baltimore. Cupid had obviously decided to take Mencken in hand, for the name of his fateful lecture, delivered with his familiar air of cynicism, was 'How to Catch a Husband'.

Mencken was born in Baltimore in 1880 and the city would remain his spiritual home. He made his name as a young journalist there, and, while not always the greatest stylist, his commitment to delivering forthright, opinionated pieces made him a household name. In 1918 he published *In Defense of Women*, an irreverent look at the dynamic that exists between the genders. Those of generous spirit chose to see the work as ironically progressive, while one critic suggested that he was in fact 'the country's high-priest of woman-haters'.

Regardless of his intentions in writing *Defense*, Mencken's demeanour, energy and intellect made him highly desirable to a number of women. But Mencken refused to submit to their attentions and was perhaps America's most famous single man in the 1920s.

Then came the invitation to address Goucher College in May 1923. Among the audience was Haart, at 24 years old eighteen years Mencken's junior and the youngest member of the faculty. She was also herself an immensely talented writer. Mencken's talk was supposed to be a wry review of *Defense*, no doubt meant to inspire debate and controversy in equal measure. Haart seems to have taken it all rather more literally. She quickly stole the previously icy heart of the critic, who described their relationship as a 'beautiful adventure'.

Their courtship lasted for seven years before they married in 1930. One paper reacted to the news with the following: 'Bachelors of the nation are aghast and sore afraid, like a sheep without a leader.'

Mencken himself said that he was superstitious, 'and always follow hunches: this one seemed to be a superb one.'

This most unexpected of love stories was to have a tragic end, though, when Sara died in 1935 from tubercular meningitis.

Addressing the problem

Arnold Gingrich was something of a publishing phenomenon, building *Esquire* magazine from nothing into a
global brand with a roster of writers that included many of
the greatest American names of the 20th century. However,
were it not for a letter turning up on his desk at just the right
moment, there's every chance that the magazine would have
been called *Stag* or even *Beau*. And with a name like either
of those, who would have backed it to become the institution
it is today?

Gingrich was born in 1903 and grew up in Grand Rapids,
Michigan. In the early 1930s, as America faced a long and
deep Depression, Gingrich saw the opportunity to set up a
new title. In partnership with David Smart, a publisher from
Chicago, he formulated a magazine that would appeal to
young, professional men, with an emphasis on strong,
original literary content.

With the printing presses ready to whirr into action on
the first edition in 1933, Gingrich and Smart had everything
in place except a snappy title. *Stag* would have been
altogether too boisterous and *Beau* too dandyish. For a while
they even considered *Trim*, which might have done for a
magazine aimed at hairdressers or body-builders but hardly
suited their vision. Then one morning in November 1932
Gingrich's secretary brought in his post. In among it was a
letter addressed to 'Arnold Gingrich, Esquire'. The lightning bolt had struck, and he realised that *Esquire* would be
the perfect name. It defined the magazine not only as for

men, but for men who commanded a certain level of respect; men of status and implicit style.

The magazine proved to be a huge success and employed writers such as Truman Capote, William Faulkner, F. Scott Fitzgerald, Ernest Hemingway, Norman Mailer, Dorothy Parker and John Steinbeck. Gingrich remained editor until the 1960s and helped create the blueprint for a great many of the men's magazines that followed it. *Esquire* continues to prosper today, with numerous international editions and a circulation in the USA alone of over three quarters of a million.

I'll have a 2,355,880

Some numbers in life are more important than others. For instance, picking your lottery numbers is a serious business. As is making your choice from a Chinese restaurant menu. One man who combined his Chinese meal and his lottery ticket was fantastically rewarded for his efforts.

Twenty-three-year-old Danny Williams, an engineer from Essex, was dining with his girlfriend at a Chinese restaurant while holidaying in Greece. At the end of their meal each was given a fortune cookie containing the usual sage advice for the reader. Williams also noticed a run of six numbers at the bottom of his particular nugget of wisdom. Having always previously selected his lottery numbers at random from week to week, he made the momentous decision that these figures should become his regular lottery picks.

They brought him moderate success, providing him with a few £10 notes along the way and, on one occasion, a not quite life-changing £36. Convinced that all six numbers would come up the week he stopped playing them, Williams remained admirably loyal to his selection. Then on the last Saturday of June in 2008 the six magic numbers – 11, 12, 22, 23, 24 and 36 – came up. Williams was one of ten winners, sharing a jackpot of £2,355,880, and so his share came out at £235,588. It's to be hoped he celebrated with a Chinese banquet.

Model aeroplanes

Kate Moss is a supermodel who has earned millions in a career that has prospered for almost twenty years. Her back-list of boyfriends is so full of celebrities that it reads like an edition of *Heat* magazine. Her story began back in 1988 with a classic case of 'right place, right time'.

Katherine Moss was born in January 1974 in Croydon, south London, an area that to the untrained eye bears little relation to the catwalk worlds of Paris, Milan and New York. Measuring around 5 feet 7 inches and a little over 7 stone, Kate was the antithesis of the curvy, statuesque specimens like Cindy Crawford and Claudia Schiffer who were the leading models of the day.

When Kate was just fourteen she was passing through New York's JFK airport en route back home from a family holiday in the Bahamas. There she caught the eye of Sarah

Doukas, one of the top bookers for the Storm Modelling Agency. Doukas saw something in the waif-like girl and signed her up. Among Moss's first jobs was an advertising campaign for Calvin Klein that helped give birth to the 'heroin chic' look of the early 1990s.

It wasn't long before her client list included the likes of Chanel, Gucci, Rimmel and Yves Saint Laurent. In more recent times, she has also developed a hugely successful and lucrative relationship with Top Shop. While her personal life has had some very public ups and downs, her roll-call of exes includes Johnny Depp, Daniel Craig and Pete Doherty. How different things might have been had her flight in 1988 been out of LaGuardia or Newark.

Coining a name

William Somerset Maugham was one of 20th-century Britain's great men of letters and, reputedly, among its highest paid. A skilled exponent of drama and long- and short-form fiction, his masterpiece is considered to be *Of Human Bondage*. It was a critical review of this work that inadvertently solved a problem for Somerset Maugham: what to call his next book?

Somerset Maugham was born in 1874 in Paris, where his father worked as a lawyer at the British embassy. He had a rather stiff and difficult upbringing, not helped by the mockery he received at school in England for his poor grasp of the language (French being his first language) and a very pronounced stutter he had developed. Set on becoming a writer, his family somewhat railroaded him into becoming a medical student at King's College London. However, the experience was to prove fruitful, for it introduced him to life as experienced by some of London's 'lower sorts' and provided a basis of knowledge for his first novel, *Liza of Lambeth*, published in 1897.

Although he continued to publish regularly, it was another ten years before his next big hit, the stage play *Lady Frederick*. Six years later came *Of Human Bondage*, the tale of Philip Carey which made heavy use of Somerset Maugham's own life. The novel took something of a critical hammering until Theodore Dreiser, an author and reviewer, suggested it was touched by genius.

The following year, Somerset Maugham travelled around the Pacific islands as he worked on a fictionalised account of the artist Paul Gauguin, who had spent many years living in Tahiti. The book was eventually published in 1919 and in naming it, the author turned to a review in the *Times Literary Supplement* of *Of Human Bondage*. Discussing Philip Carey, the reviewer had written: 'Like so many young men, he was so busy yearning for the moon, that he never saw the six-pence at his feet.' Somerset Maugham decided to call his Gauguin novel *The Moon and Sixpence*. It was among the best received of all his works.

Nonetheless, Somerset Maugham remained his own harshest critic, summing himself up in later years as 'in the very first row of the second-raters'.